ICONOLOGIA

ICONOLOGIA

LEONARD BASKIN

Harcourt Brace Jovanovich, Publishers
San Diego   New York   London

ISBN 0-15-143560-X

Printed in Great Britain

First United States edition

For Lisa
&
for Sidney
&
John & Jose
&
Max
&
for Ted
My critical claque

Contents

A disclaiming and averring note

All books tend to have, either craftily hidden or boldly present, an exculpatory note, disclaiming this or averring that: this book is, alas, no exception. I can but speculate as to why I have been put to the ardent making of homages to artists of the past, and in inordinate numbers. It is not, I feel certain, an act of simple or complex, straightforward or devious, obeisance, from a poor contemporary thing to the titans of the past: I suffer in myself no false humility. Rather, this near-blizzard of portraits-in-homage is the anxiety-obsessed wail emitted by an artist who feels isolated and under siege. It is the stretched, the harassed call for comrades-in-arms, for reinforcing help and fighting strength, for justification, for reassurance, a battering on the door of history to send witnesses to plead his cause, to usurp the enemies who have so wantonly seized power and control. Is this absurd posturing? Is it the framing of an outlandish rationale for the obvious and manifest pleasure in the making of portraits?; but I had dearly and long ago learned the truism that there is no arguing with feeling. Whatever the reality, I feel, since the death of Rico Lebrun, entirely alone, as though drifting in an alien, an unknown sea. I do not feel weak or even threatened, but I do feel alone. No living artist allegorically shares with me the long and silent hours in my studio. I know that I do not struggle alone, that others valiantly, heroically and relentlessly struggle against the engulfing tidal-wave of know-nothing avant-gardism; but I feel alone. And that irrational and unarguable feeling of isolation is the spur that causes me to seek allies in the ranks of dead artists. And if not as the rendering of homages, then for the building of a protective buttress that one ransacks the past. Why, I wonder, the replication of certain portraits? How many Barlachs? What constitutes a sufficiency in Eakins-icons? Powerful ties of identification must fuel the making of many portraits of a single artist. Blake and Bresdin along with Barlach and Eakins are artists I have depicted in sculpture, drawings and prints. Barlach was in the purest sense a paradigm, the modern sculptor who spoke most directly and cogently to my desperate needs; Eakins for the glorious monumentality of his work, but more succinctly for the strength and passion of his beliefs, and for his

1

prideful stance against the yapping stupidity of his philistinistic attackers; Blake for being a channel into poetry and printing and all of the private and public vices pertaining thereto; and Bresdin, for whom I felt a simple, deep affection – and my multiplying his image was a further expression of my delight in his work and in the amassing of a collection of his mysterious drawings and prints, and in my small role in furthering his renown. Thus, the making of artist's portraits is, in part, the declaration of homage and, in another larger part, the clutching unto one's bosom of historical imperatives and exemplars and, in an infantile way, indulging in image-making as a magical rite, vainly desiring to imbibe and inculcate into oneself the character, quality and genius of the artist displayed.

Eakins. we. 1966.

2

Thomas Eakins

Of the innumerable objects that litter the surfaces of my quotidian
ambience, none can be counted as sacrosanct except a scuffed and
soiled old cigar-box, which is a treasured reliquary holding relics of
Thomas Eakins; in that dim topless box, which was once his, rest
several of the red wax-topped pins that are deployed, like battalions
on a vast plain in an old military book, in his perspective drawings:
and two small brushes, magical tools now for having been in Eakins's
hand, they are directly redolent of the painter and they bespeak, those
two tiny brushes, an age of minute concern with the detail of aspect
and habilement; that scarred tobacco-box also contains an odd home-
made pen, encrusted with wax which secures its strange nib (Eakins
wrote a beautiful, easy-flowing version of copperplate, a hand taught
to him by his father, Benjamin, who was a scribe). What did Eakins
draw or write with that pen? And beyond all of these, there is a small
brazen set of dividers, well-made and well-worn. Relics are devices of
veneration. Indeed, I venerate Thomas Eakins, America's greatest
painter. But I own no relics of Copley or of Heade or of Church, or of
the sculptors Rimmer and Saint-Gaudens, all in their manners and
metiers the very near-equal of Eakins. No, it is not the paintings,
despite the Rembrandtesque grandeur of their realism, that lifts Eakins
apart; it is rather the perceptible actuality of his indomitable spirit, as
he moved through his inhospitable world, arraying his time and place
with masterworks, despite the near-universal scouring stupidity and
aberrant mis-appreciation. Yes, it is the man's life and his unequaled
soul-diminishing struggle to preserve his artistic probity. His
forbearance was stoutly dignified at the braying of prurient prudes
and he held fast against the onslaughts of privileged philistinism. His
friend, Walt Whitman, said of him, "Tom Eakins is not a painter, he's
a force." It was a life, that is, a career of near-total denigration, brutish
indifference and neglect. The searing effects of this lapse in patronage,
this national deficiency in judgement, this fundamental want of
understanding, can be clearly read in his face as its furrows deepen,
the flesh tightens over facial bone, its creases sink into crevices, its
look of bewildered but deep hurt becoming fixed, its lines running
towards a tragic configuration. Eakins was not entirely alone; his loyal

3

Eakins: 1885. etching. [Detail]. 1950.

and talented wife Susan was a classic instance of devotion; she was a buttress, comrade, lover: a few alert critics championed his work. A large number of his pupils revered him, posed for him, swam with him, set up an academy for him, became very close to him, the young sculptor Samuel Murray becoming a virtual son to him. Eakins was innocent of fancy; his perception of the world was adamantine in its palpable directness, plainness, ordinariness. He accepted the evidence of his senses; he was the arch-American realist trying to paint what he saw. But he was Eakins, touched by Rembrandt and Velasquez. And in the alembic that was his palette, the simple oarsman and plain net-menders are trapped in a landscape of frozen time and extenuated space. The distressing element in Eakins's paintings was its honesty; it had naught of the preferred dishonesty of sentimentalism, wildly current in his time. His portraits touch into deep and veiled recesses of his sitters' personae; the women are almost always profoundly tragic with deep, inward-searching eyes, the visages in the deepest melancholia, the men rigidly monumental, clothed in golden light. His sitters were in the greater number alarmed at the revelatory depictions and tended not to return to the Mt Vernon Street studio, forcing Eakins to abandon the pictures. His ''The Gross Clinic'', perhaps the great American painterly masterwork, was exhibited in the medical section of the Chicago 1890s World Fair instead of the Hall of Art (or whatever its banal name was), as it was judged offensive to the American sensibility! (See Mrs Trollope and see Dickens et alia, in re that species of sensibility.) Dr S. Gross, a distinguished surgeon and teacher of his day, who would be forgotten but for the fame attached to Eakins's portrait of him, his colleagues and students, does not mention Eakins, nor the historic event of the creation of ''The Gross Clinic'' in his two-volume autobiography. Eakins was quite continuously attacked by crippling know-nothing fat-headedness. He was dismissed from his cherished post as head of painting at the Pennsylvania Academy of Fine Arts, because his passion for honesty and probity caused him to reveal the genitals of a male model before a mixed-class of young men and women. The ferocious struggle that ensued (that bruised priggish sensibility again) which revealed a streak of religious zealotry in a branch of his family and exposed the crude opportunism of a trusted student, further deepened and darkened his

Eakins: etching. 1964.

Eakins: 1870. etching. 1950.

visage. Three American museums bought paintings from Eakins in his lifetime. Albert Barnes, the Argyrol king and prescient collector of Renoir, Cezanne at al., paid Eakins $5,000 for his large oil study of Dr Agnew for the "Anatomy of Dr Agnew"; that sum which came to Eakins c. 1905 represented more than the totality of his lifelong earnings from painting. It was a benefice to us and to the generations that surround us, that Benjamin Eakins left his son that fine house and a sufficiency to carry on with life's needs. But Eakins was combatively exuberant, buttressed with mighty reserves of strength, immensely alive to an intense joie de vivre; a photograph shows him thrusting his heavy, old, nude body into a crashing wave, somewhere on the Jersey coast; that joyous photograph displays the undiminished surviving Eakins. That force which Whitman specified was promethean, unstoppable, impervious, ever onward-flowing; and yet a photograph taken of him in 1907 reveals a stricken Eakins, the invisible Eakins of this ghastly story: the superbly successful John Singer Sargent while visiting Philadelphia was asked by his rich, socially secure, all-knowing hostess, "Is there anyone at all you'd like to meet in Philadelphia?", "Well," replied Sargent, "there's Eakins, for instance." "Who's Eakins?" said the hostess. Eakins was interested in the sciences; he scattered scientific apparatus in the portraits of the physicists, chemists, etc. (his friends, usually). He dwelt with interested care on the depiction of specific instruments and laboratory paraphernalia, but more critical were his significant contributions to the evolvement of the cinema. Thomas Eakins used photography as an adjunct to his pursuit of reality, using photographs as an aide-memoire for his painting, but inevitably the photographs emerge as artifacts, meritorious in their own right. How remarkable that the special luminous honesty that pervades Eakins's paintings suffuses the subjects in his photographs. There is a notebook in a private Philadelphia collection, kept by Eakins as a journal of work begun, when finished, etc.; in it he lists all of his possessions; on several pages he numerates the furniture, looking-glasses, cutlery, dishes, candle-sticks, nails, nuts, bicycle, studio impedimenta: the list ends with, "and a house full of pictures that no one wants".

Eakins: 1895. etching. 1950.

Augustus Saint-Gaudens

Like Noah, Saint-Gaudens was great in his generation. A seemingly endless, thin and barren sculptural time stretches from the canny but convincing naiveté of Rush to Saint-Gaudens; the stony inanities and marble mediocrities (the odd co-mingling of Yankee greenbacks and Roman carving) are momentarily forgotten in the deep, stirring works of J. Q. A. Ward and the mighty figures of William Rimmer. We will not pause to note the occasional, the fragmentary achievements of an O'Connor, a Bessie Vonnah, or the youthful MacMonnies. Working to commission is akin to working within the confines of a restrictive form, such as a classic sonnet; its dialectical vectors are both simultaneously freeing and constricting. In this age artists are busily engaged as small-time manufacturers, producing goods whose value is overwhelmingly "conspicuous". I rather imagine that Saint-Gaudens and sculptors of his day saw themselves, if not quite as utilitarian as architects, indubitably as close working adjuncts to them. Indeed, nineteenth-century sculptors had close professional associations with architects and their firms: thus Saint-Gaudens's relationship with McKim, Mead and White, who supplied architectural surrounds and fundaments, bases and sockels for many of Saint-Gaudens's statues. Rodin, Saint-Gaudens's contemporary, produced bronzes to suit his fancy and was dependent on the monied sensibilities of connoisseurs and of "the knowing ones". Thus the working to commissions, to the often-ignorant and very often offensive opinions of committee members, to the restrictive elements of available monies and wrong-headed notions, all of that; but one was free of the Rodinesque necessity of peddling one's wares, hoping for positive judgement, subtle taste, and ready cash. Saint-Gaudens's commissioned Lincoln brings to mind that other Washington-based Lincoln. Is this the place to consider the astonishing space that Henry Bacon provided for Daniel French's huge portrait of Lincoln? Think of that statue sitting in front of a Federal Court House or, if one can manage it, transform the statue into a Secretary of War or of a weighty Solon; we render it in our imaginations as vulgar and banal, inevitably turgid. It is of course our attitude toward Lincoln, our awe and love of Columbia's martyr, that lifts all portrayals of him beyond our critical capacities. We have

A. St Gaudens. lithograph. 1982.

no disinterested approach to Lincoln. The weight of his personality and the myth of his death blur our assessing judgements. Place then a large sculpture done with exemplary skills, a naturalistic portrayal of Lincoln, drenched, as is inevitable, with our near worshipful love, into a temple, sufficient of scale and with an amplitude of space, empty of all else but the simulacrum of the mythical figure, his most famous words engraved into the deep silences of the surrounding walls. A magical experience ensues. The issue of these interactions is trance-like, the workings of these interconnecting elements is unlike any other American public sculptural experience, as indeed Lincoln remains unique, the embodiment of the American archetypal hero; sprung from backwoods loins, grand of stature, apprehendable, lovable of person, savior of his nation, and murdered: the expressed national grief of that martyrdom still reverberates in us. Saint-Gaudens's Lincoln, wanting a hallowed space, does not, as sculpture, deeply affect us; the figure is grave, magisterial, solemn in its contemplative posture, but it does not enkindle our deepest sympathies, we do not respond to forms that could and should hold mythic power, because these forms are wanting. No, not for that austere meditative Lincoln; nor for his Diana, however lithesome, lissome, darling, divine and daring she may be as she treads the very air; nor for his Farragut, uneasily landbound on sea-legs; not even for his Nike-led Sherman, so pertinaciously driving against all currents, across the open spaces that betoken the onset of Central Park; no, for none of these, but I esteem and extol Saint-Gaudens for the prodigious memorial to Colonel Shaw and to his immortal black troops, of whom too many perished at the "Battle of Fort Wagner", and for his numerous and masterly bronze reliefs, portraits of savants, artists, friends, and portraits of their children. The bas-relief, especially the very low relief, is a highly difficult and problematical medium, as it precariously exists between painting and sculpture, wanting the quintessential strength of each, the color of painting and the three-dimensionality of sculpture. The modeler in low-relief must perforce use all of the illusion-building devices of drawing to achieve a spatial ambience in which the figures can live; the sculptor through the use of further illusionistic tricks suggests the roundness of the figures. Saint-Gaudens was the master of this awesomely complex and difficult medium, was privy to the stringent means of exceedingly subtle modeling. Consider his life-enhanced portraits of William Dean Howells and his daughter in deep converse, as an instance; how gracefully and felicitously and with what comeliness the two figures swell the space of this very small plaquette. How surely and with what swift certainty Howells and his daughter Mildred are personalized and their characters adduced and elegantly set forth. And this so perfectly achieved in a tiny compass; think of the immense Robert Louis Stevenson at St Giles, and all of the studies and smaller versions of the bed-ridden writer, pillowed to a half-upright position, cigarette and pen in his hands, intent only on work. The relief is unforgettable, it rests solidly in one's memory, one recalls it instantly, and it supersedes all other images in Stevenson's large iconography. And there are many other memorable portraits magically achieved in the lowest of relief: of Asa Grey, for instance, the forward-looking botanist in a sympathetic portrayal, enchanting for the subtlety of its modeling; and Bastien-Lepage, the French painter who teaches us the greatness of Millet by the example of his sentimentalizing peasant subjects, but very spry and lively in Saint-Gaudens's subtle realization; and a host of others, women, men, and children. Committees for the Shaw Memorial came into being, dispersed and regrouped, but Augustus Saint-Gaudens would not hurry his great task to completion. One is reminded of Flaubert's response to Maxime Du Camp's endless hectoring to finish his novel and hurry to Paris, where chances were being preempted by other, lesser talents. Flaubert passionately and irately wrote inter alia, "Let the United States perish, before I rush to completion a single sentence" of *Madame Bovary*. Saint-Gaudens would not be hurried. From the simplest beginning conception, preserved in a drawing, Saint-Gaudens slowly evolved, in degrees and steps and stages ever more complex, ever more encompassing, the final design of the memorial. From what was little more than a high-relief of Colonel Shaw, the piece developed in geometric leaps. It bespeaks Saint-Gaudens's finest impulses that drove him into greater and ever greater complexity, that he should be endlessly dissatisfied with his earlier macquettes; and the continuously expanding sketches reveal his desire to enlarge the meanings and implications of his commission. The naturalness of involving and including the brave soldiers of the

11

Fifty-Fourth Regiment was logical and inevitable; the concept of the monument grew in complexity, in scale and grandeur. By thus casting together the Colonel and his black soldiers, Saint-Gaudens grapples with history itself instead of with the memory of a single person, granted the splendor, even nobility, of his character. In our age of easy and great and significant distortion, the problems presented by the marching men could have been more easily resolved: Saint-Gaudens had no option but to dispose those boring legs enclosed in dreadful formless trousers, but trousers withal, not pantaloons nor knickerbockers, and shoes, specific US Army issue and in serried marching ranks: poor sculptors, however inventive the rhythms, or even syncopated the arrangement or organization, they remain a heavy, dour, insoluble problem; as are Prince Albert coats and waistcoats with a plurality of buttons, and neckties and pockets. One might add all the habiliments of civilized humans, but especially of men: it is the stuff of sculptural nightmare, but Saint-Gaudens does as well as his century, his mode, his manner allowed; he makes the feet and the legs move as rhythmically as possible. It is no accident that the most pleasurable public statuary is either entirely nude, as is Derwent Woods's "David" at Hyde Park Corner, or a figure swathed in imaginary drapery, as the Princess Alexandria memorial by Alfred Gilbert. Those endless commemorative sculptures of historical personages exist visibly hidden in our largest cities, and when we do come upon a Webster or a Sumner or a Peter Cooper, we either turn embarrassedly away, or wish the corpulent frock-coated gents in moldy green would disappear, or at least take off their clothing. The savant said, "Ils faut être de son temps." Indeed, but what a burden that often inflicts. The affliction of contemporary clothes has led to bizarre sculptural resolutions: wrap them up in togas, Romanize them all. Rodin does not have Balzac's great belly pressing against a many-buttoned waistcoat. Rodin escapes these problems of horrid costume by swathing Balzac's mighty corpulence in a timeless nightgown. In France and Britain the annual exhibitions at the Salon and the Academy provided a venue for sculptors to exhibit small and larger bronzes designed to please themselves, to express their vertu, to communicate their commitment to a school or a tendency or a new movement; and the burgeoning of Romanticism and Symbolism, along

13

with the pervasive and unyielding Beaux Arts academicism, saw the inevitable proliferation of a host of small bronzes, very personal and often capricious. Those annual shows were also events at which all sculptors exhibited plaster versions of their current monumental commissions. The ubiquitous reducing and enlarging machines, used in both carving and bronze casting, did considerable damage to sculptural intentions. Virtually all of the nineteenth-century sculptors multiplied their works, using these insensitive mechanical devices; versions in all sizes exist of what may prove the nineteenth century's greatest sculptural monument, Rodin's "Bourgeois de Calais". Saint-Gaudens's greatest monument, "The Shaw Memorial", exists in only one size, the size in which Saint-Gaudens modeled it; he sent a full-size plaster model of it to the Paris Salon of 1900 (before which Rodin doffed his hat). Smaller versions of several of Saint-Gaudens's larger public works exist, viz., the Springfield Puritan, the Diana, the Lincoln, and doubtless others. I do not know of any Saint-Gaudens equivalents to the personal bronzes of his English and French contemporaries. The portrait reliefs are essentially private. Editions were cast of studies, bozzetti, macquettes, etc. How fortunate we are to have arrived at a time that has swallowed all previous time, that it is reasonable to "épater l'avante guarde"; and to devise a style and a manner decanted from all available and known styles: the times, they are confusing, conflicting and confounding. The gift of near-endless choice is cacophonous and very difficult, but wondrously enriching; we can and do host all of the world's makings. That massive inheritance is at our fingertips in the form of photo-indices; an iconography of limitless possibility at one's instantaneous behest: anything goes. It is Saint-Gaudens's genius that allows him to overcome the sculptural limitations of his time and place. Shaw and his troops drive indomitably forward and onwards, they are compositionally bound and ideologically fused to their purpose. The greatness of the memorial, beyond the wonderful particularization of the troops (my friend Professor Sidney Kaplan, who has written revealingly anent this memorial, its sources, its making and its implications, found in one of Saint-Gaudens's old storage sheds at Cornish a series of beautiful heads, studiously and subtly modeled from life, studies of the marching black soldiers, eloquently testifying

15

A. St Gaudens. relief, bronze. 1981.

to his struggle to individualize the soldiers, to make them entirely free of stereotypes) and the felt humaneness in their depiction and in the sympathetic depiction of Shaw, is the great sense of their being bonded, togethered, driving as one towards Fort Wagner; their inexorable march to their deaths, their manifest, declared desire to militarily serve, unto death, in a war against slavery. A whirlwind of motivated movement, led on by a flying, if somewhat cramped, Nike; the monument memorializes a fine and great moment in a war beset by corruption, selflessness, greed, heroism, counter-purposes, bravery, stupidity, indomitability, cupidity. And no American war, no battle in any American war, and no combatants in any engagement in any American war have been so splendidly memorialized. Saint-Gaudens's long and ardent labor reached to the deepest levels of fruition in this beautiful and magnificent work.

George Fuller

There is a dreamy, misted, tremulous, opalescent aura, overlaying the landscape and overhanging the people in George Fuller's paintings. It is as though veils of mystifying vapor intercede between painted object and our capacity to perceive them. His figures are all wrapped in translucent umbras, suggesting in a critic's recent words "a materialization of spirit". This mature style was a resulting distillation over many years of the paintings that moved him most during his crucial year, 1860, in Europe. During the long decades of farming, which his father's death and the salvaging of the family fortune demanded, those Rembrandts and Millets and Monticellis must have loomed ever larger in his consciousness and were crucial for his final enrichment and evolvement of his mature manner and mode. They must have spun and abraded each other, the remembered canvases, grinding into the fine evanescent dust that Fuller spread like a murky illumination over his paintings. I have a powerful and continuing image of the long distillative years in which Fuller's bright obscurantism developed in his memory and in his desire to paint, and during the long winters and Sundays, when painting was possible. The crop-burgeoned fields in the Connecticut Valley at Deerfield, where the Fuller family farm was located, yielded beyond its principal crop of broad-leaf shade-grown tobacco, a configuration and a locus for Fuller's paintings of landscape, plain and peopled. Fuller is the master of half-lights, his universe is but dimly perceived, as though a continuous crepuscular scrim has been drawn across the face of nature. His bitumen-drenched paintings have doubtless darkened, which has further obscured the delicate translucence that Fuller favored. The great art historian Wolfgang Stechow, upon seeing a Fuller landscape of the Deerfield area, its hillocks and treetops singed in gold by the setting sun, all the rest lost, absorbed into the gathering darkness, said, "It is like a late Rembrandt," – despite the incessant caviling of the canting-crew, led by Royal Cortissoz, who when praising Fuller did so with unfailing reference to his supposed academic weaknesses. They aver that despite his massive lacks, he manages a quality of "purest poetry"; they allude to some supernatural capacity, an indescribable entity which allows Fuller to

George Fuller. drawing. 1987.

18

achieve works of indisputable beauty. Rot and nonsense. Fuller was a bold and original painter, with a haphazard, an unconventional training, but he was trained; he also had oddities, singularities, an eccentric vision which permitted him to develop into the artist whose near-unique voice we cherish today. His was an eccentric vision, in which edges are expunged and lines dismissed. In Mumford's acute words, "What are Fuller's pictures? His later work . . . all suggests that nostalgia for beauty that haunted and plagued the severe Puritan mind. He gave in to the desire, and in the act of painting did his best to suppress it. Nothing comes out of the background sharply and boldly; but the world is seen through a pervasive mist, vague, tender, in which the forms are evanescent and the atmosphere is stable." Fuller's contained passion was the deep lambency that shone from the depths of his subjects. That light is an interior luminence that lights up mysteriously and enigmatically the hidden depths of personality, the covert roots of character and the indistinct lineaments of individuality. There is an unmistakable and palpable ache, a miasma of melancholy that lifts off Fuller's paintings of "The Quadroon" and of "Gypsy Women", and a perceptible disquietude in all of Fuller's work. Fuller had made three trips through the slave-sodden South, recording in sketchbooks and small watercolors the life in field or cabin; he vividly limned the slaves in the actuality of their slavery and he is virtually the only Northern artist of note, quite possibly the only artist, to draw American blacks in the South before the Civil War. Those sketchbooks are national treasure, they are relics of lived history. His later portrayals of young women, trapped by birth into pools of resentment, distrust and hatred, are rooted in those youthful years spent in Alabama and Georgia. The half-figures tend to thrust at the viewer with a frontal directness that is belied by the equivocating quality of the light which emanates from the figures. A strange resonating tension develops in the contrast between the seeming straightforwardness of position and posture and the halting qualities of muted fulgence. The extreme subtlety of Fuller's touch and approach deepen the levels of ambiguity that wraps like a costume around his fuliginous personages.

Rico Lebrun

Rico Lebrun, like the Swiss Hans Erni and the Brazilian Candido
Portinari, suffered the absurd burden of superfluity of talent; unlike
them he overcame that cursèd blessing. Additionally he was crushed
by that omnipresent heritage of great art that sits like a malicious
suffocating incubus on the aspirations of young Italian and other
European artists. The Florentine painter Renzo Grazzinni recounted to
me the perilous enrichment of playing ball about and against Santa
Croce, even to chasing a rogue ball·into that hallowed ground, the
Giottos aglow and aglower at the intrusion. And the back-breaking
weight of prevalent Massaccios and Donatellos and Michelangelos,
and the generational layers of genius stretching on and on to one's
peril, staying one's gesture, halting the naturalness of impulse, and
demanding Heraclean strength to persist in the face of that
mountainous achievement. The vast flood of inexpensive photographic
reproductions has tended to universalize that situation and, however
remote an artist may be situated from the actual monuments, their
photographic simulacra seep into one's consciousness, bidden or not.
That overwhelming ponderance of images of past works of art is a
crucial new phenomenon in the passage and transference of influence.
That pictorial plethora is simultaneously enslaving and liberating. At
the age of eighteen Lebrun could draw with the consummacy of a
Renaissance master, and alas, did: it required a half-lifetime to rid
himself of those restrictive gifts and of those destructive endowments.
In overcoming the Renaissance influence Lebrun fell under the yoking
spell of Picasso; he was blinded by the radiance of "Guernica". The
genius of Lebrun showed through even in the habiliment of influence,
and during the time of this dependence he created wonderful works,
culminating with the "Crucifixion Triptych". The series of paintings of
exhausted, disused and worn-out reaping, harrowing, harvesting,
plowing and baling tools, here all rusted-red flowering within decayed
orange, menacing in the cool-green glades and grass; these images of
dead machines, baring their blades, their hooks, their formidable
spikes and claws loom as isolated menacing forms in the anxiety-
shredding decade of World War Two. The principal work of that time
and the very large number of preparatory and related works was the

20

Rico Lebrun. drawing. 1985.

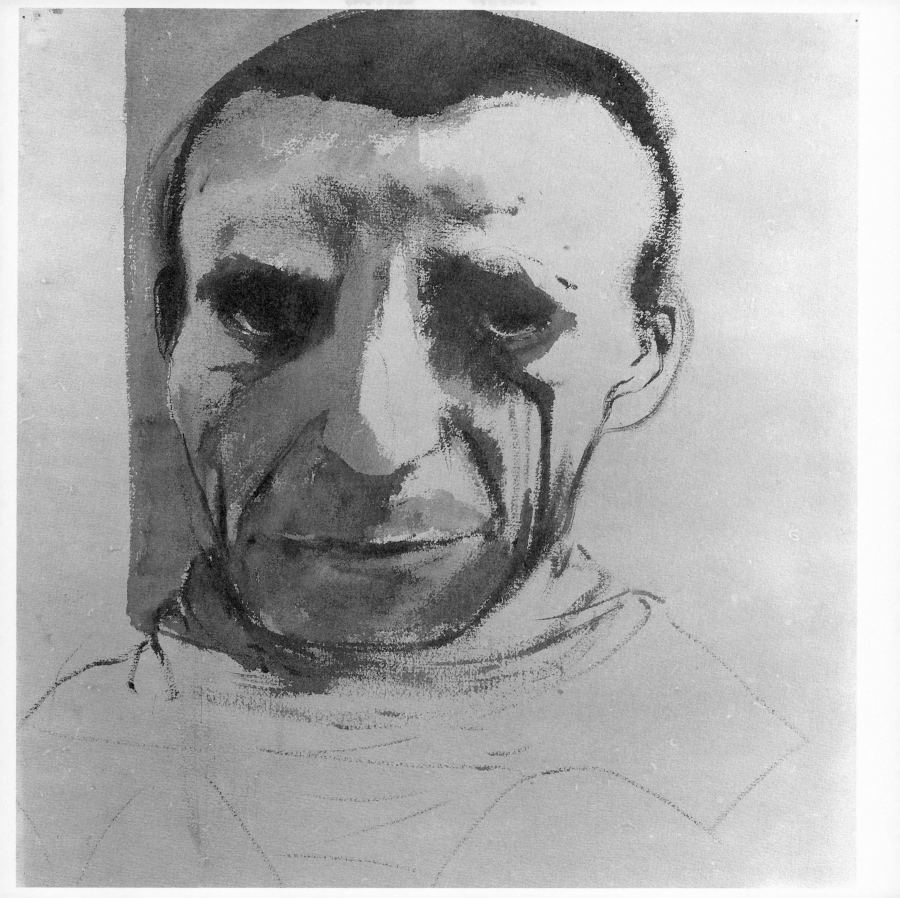

immense triptych of the crucifixion which is housed at Syracuse University. Lebrun thrusts us directly into the tragic dimension of Christ's death, of Mary's expiring dolor, of John's proffer of solace, of the Magdalene's prostrate finger-wrung penance and the hulking predatory presence of the Centurions. Lebrun painted many versions of these participants in Golgotha's black night of terror, terrifying images of the Virgin in the gasps and spasms of unendurable grief and the Centurions, now like monstrous armored creatures of another time, and again, clad in grotesque suits of armor of a primordial bearing armed with halberds. But the mighty triptych is marred by Lebrun's dependency on Picasso, a bizarre case of artist self-blindness; of Lebrun using specific Guernician ideograms, for a hand, and other borrowings. But Lebrun doubtless had deep inklings of his Picassoid disorder (a specter – Picasso – is haunting Europe and the world); for he departed to Mexico and spent a year or more, making huge abstract collages, and there was redemption in that cutting and gluing; he cleansed his style: he flushed Picasso away. In that strenuous year of self-confrontation he drained off all the extraneous and reductive elements that had lessened the impact of his genius and finally the untrammeled, the uncorrupted, the true Rico Lebrun emerged. And for near a decade, the hot essence of Lebrun, unalloyed, boiled and raged and spilled into the wondrous vessels that are his glory. That percolation spewed works that expose the outlines of human decay and human disorder, of humanity steeped in a frozen wasteland that is genocidal, greedy and rapinous, the terrifying exhaustion of war, the constant, soul-destroying malice of these times. The words written by Michael Levey about Goya are pertinent to Lebrun, who of all contemporary artists is kin to Goya: "Goya's art is seriously concerned with the fate of mankind, . . . and he sees mankind within the social framework . . . Goya kept humanity as his central concern. . . ." Like Goya, Lebrun in his mighty last years found the generative impulses that animated his art in the darker, catastrophic side of human life: thus the Holocaust was a subject which he insisted no serious artist could neglect, in such terrifying paintings as "Buchenwald Cart" heaped with humans now reduced to remnants, now but bony relics, and "Study for Dachau Chamber" in which figures fly into the cremating ovens of Auschwitz and Dachau.

22

Lebrun confronts the mind-curdling reality of the least human of human endeavors, and in paintings and drawings of dissolution, dismemberment and incineration he is saying, all is not vanity, all is horror. Although Lebrun painted his entire life, and in his last two years made many sculptures, his ultimate mastery was in his drawings. Throwing his probing net of lines and washes very wide, Lebrun made in his last decade a mass of drawings for Dante's *Inferno* and Brecht's *Threepenny Novel*. Lebrun was sensible to the enduring relevance of great texts and he dredges them to discover an abundance of themes; revelatory and exculpatory. How he quickens to the huge task of illuminating Dante's *Inferno*: we descend with Dante and with Lebrun, down into the ever narrowing circles of Hell, in which the doomed flail and howl, scratch and bite, filling their bleak pits of abandonment with cries and shrieks made palpable with the viscosity of terror. How trenchantly Lebrun sets the miserables before us; here the figures clearly perceived in sharp delineating drawing, the line moving with masterly inevitability, snaring those figures' contours as they contort in the hallucinated pastures of the possessed: and other figures but dimly seen, lost as they are in the gloom and doom and shade in the fastnesses of damnation, their forms swell into visibility and shrink away into only partial noticeability. "Drawing," Lebrun has said, "should be, above all, not a thing of art, but a tool for understanding." The hulking, brooding, massive shapes of figures, "without the chatter of details, are clearer to me as forms and mute drama . . .". Reminiscent of Whistler's evocation of Thames-side warehouses and mill houses in that special dimness of a Victorian London night, Lebrun sees " . . . early in the morning the garbage pails, cars, gas pumps, trees, have a look of breathless beings surprised on a terrain of solemn truce before the day comes. And when I get to the studio I sit for a while in the dark watching the animal furniture . . . emerge from the lagoon of the floor." The looming singularity of his figures whether alone or coupled or in groups; their volumetric assertiveness, their overweening quality as monoliths, as dolmanic humans; so magnanimous, so broad, so chthonian the forms, so ample the shapes, that Lebrun's turning to the three dimensionality of sculpture was irresistible and near inevitable. It was with his last strengths that he undertook the

23

arduous work of making sculpture. With the selfless help of two
younger artists guiding and aiding him through the technical arcana
and manipulative necessities, Lebrun was able to work large sheets
of wax into shapes perforated and overlaid, compact and distressed,
simple and complex, all infused with that particular
Lebrunesque puissance, all redolent of his lifelong passion for the
human figure. It was that dominant passion, that began early and
never ceased, that implacable commitment to the human form that
pervades his sculptures, vitalizes and inspires them: in 1932 he wrote,
" . . . knowledge of the facts of the human form, plastically translated
into terms of its own image and likeness, is still an unexplored field
and the only realm proper to that if imagemaking." In 1959, twenty-
seven years later, with heightened fervor, he writes, " . . . the
vertebrate marvel has new sight for new eyes. Its terrain cannot be
prefabricated by geometry, nor found through bizarre accident, it may,
now and then, condescend to be measured by love." I was and am
profoundly moved by Rico Lebrun, his life and work. We were friends
and collaborated on one Gehenna book. That he has not risen to
universal esteem and admiration is undiluted evidence of the dire
disjointedness of our time, the hideous miasmal blindness that an
entrenched avant-garde, buttressed by an endlessly powerful vested
interest, can cast over our society. Recently a critic for *The New York
Times* (an intelligent one) wrote, "Rico Lebrun is so obviously a major
artist that his lack of wider fame seems almost a wilful repression on
the part of the tastemakers. He had the impoliteness to feel strongly,
respect tradition and reject novelty as invention." "The human form is
a fiery forge," wrote William Blake, and Lebrun is inseparable from his
work. Bound together and forever are the tempest, the fire and the
fury of his dedicated, deeply human achievement.

Orozco. monotype. 1985.

José Clemente Orozco

At another time, when my constructs, solutions, depositions, and resolutions of the worlds artistic and social complexities were simpler and founded in deepest ideals and hopes, I had formulated the following proposition: "Picasso was the world's greatest artist and José Clemente Orozco was the world's greatest painter." What, in that other time's innocence, I meant was that Picasso was artistry incarnate: it is inconsequential whether one likes this or that, he was the veritable spark of creativity, spontaneously generating the styles, the modes, the manner of his explosive age: the mass of indifferent, unresolved, autonomic works from his prodigious hands is an irrelevancy in the face of the staggering grandeur of his genius. Orozco, thank heavens, was wanting in that species of Picasso's "grandezza", worked within the liberating confines of an aroused self-critical apparat (if Picasso possessed even a shred of self-criticism, he would not have produced four or five wretched paintings per night in the years following the liberation of Paris). But Picasso's position is unassailable; he is the quicksilver, the golden-tipped gnomen, the phoenix of his age; Orozco is the titan whose vision was singular, monumental and consistent. The mercury in his temperament was the boiling point of tyranny; his life's work was infused with a detestation of corrupt power, a ferocious hatred of fascism, dictators, and of the usurpation of the people's right, of the despoliation of their patrimony. The long struggle for Mexican independence and freedom saw the execution of Maximillian by Juarez (can we forgive the infantilism of Brian Ahern and Paul Muni?) and climaxes with the toppling of Porfiro Diaz. And the proliferation of paintings on Mexico's public walls was an artistic accompaniment to the revolutionary zeal of Zapata, Villas and Cardenas. Lenin's dictum that the cinema is the art form of the future, and prevalent assertions of the death of easel painting, are especially crucial within the context of the flowering of Mexican walls, the recrudescence of fresco painting and the deployment of the public mural as a kind of pictorial literacy program. Three cardinal artists arose out of the mass of painters engaged in this, the first communally generated and directed painting since the earliest Renaissance; these three smote public awareness with a clanging clamor: they were Rivera, Siqueros and Orozco. Of the three Orozco is the artist of universal stature and commands our wondering attention, for here is Giotto, Masaccio, Signorelli redivivus. Orozco's painterly path never falters as he moves from one gigantic wall to another. His style slowly changes from forms that are monolithic and massively monumental to forms that in the end are more Expressionist, more personal and more sensuous. Thus he undergoes a distinct passage from the immobile monumentalities of the Preparatory School to the febrile monumentalities of Guadalajara. In the early Thirties Orozco was in Hanover, New Hampshire, where in the basement of Baker Library at Dartmouth College he executed what is incontestably the greatest wallpainting in the United States of America. The theme of the great series of frescos relates to the successive waves of conquest, defeats and renewed conquest as invaders succeeded invaders as the history of the New World, the Americas, unfolded. Beginning with the Incas, resolutely erect and striding forward, toward other panels portraying pre-Columbian Indian myth and mode; human sacrifice and the coming of Quetzelcoatl; the arrival of Cortez and the continuing destructiveness, moving on to modern times, excoriating war and capitalism; a horrifying vision of dead academicism in the form of a skeletal woman in robes giving birth to an academically-robed fetal skeleton, the parturition occurring on a bed of old folios and quartos, the attendant physicians are ranged behind, decked out in the robes of the world's most venerable and distinguished universities. The final convulsive and terrifying panel shows the risen Christ, all in yellows and reds, chopping down with a great axe the cross of the Crucifixion; synthesizing the connective theme of civilized birth and death and of humankind's continual ongoing. In Orozco's words, "The American continental peoples are now becoming aware of their own personality as it emerges from the two cultural currents, the indigenous and the European. The great American myth of Quetzelcoatl is a living one, embracing both elements and pointing clearly by its prophetic nature, to the responsibilities shared equally by the two Americas of creating here an authentic American civilization." Orozco's concentrated, compacted control is without ready comparison; he is a consummate draughtsman and we move from panel to panel apprehending the

Orozco. monotype. 1985.

great work. Orozco is the master orchestrater; making harmony out of divers means, he melds the narratival necessities, the pictorial means, the overriding content into a whole that is larger than its parts. Of course, each panel is not equally successful, nor does each move us equally; nor does Giotto's, but the totality is overwhelming. The young Orozco begins his artistic enterprise with a series of very free, very loose, very sensual watercolors (the most intimate of painterly mediums) of whores in bordellos, often brutal in caricaturing the lascivious spectacle, and often tender, but never condescends to be sentimental: he moves with his times to larger, more public formulations. When the flame of his political passion was fullest and purest, when his hopes for the revolution were highest, Orozco covered the immense wall of the Preparatory School with an immensity of fresco images that enlarge and expand our understanding. Orozco is pervasively monumental. Life is never decorative in necessity. Before our marveling eyes we see the amalgam of peasant, soldier and worker, forging a new trinitarian power: soldiers in a phalanx, a forward moving, crushing, bruising, unyielding frontal assault; and women, pyramidal in their stoniness, sit in the timeless postures of mourning, or accompanying the soldiers, as in "Soldaderas" and "Return to the Battlefield"; or resolute as "Women of the Workers". At the Preparatory School Orozco's style is tight, the outlines acting as rigid containers of form. As he moved from wall to enormous wall, his style eased, the outline lost its fierce bounding and binding rôle, grew less tense, became freer, and finally the outline, if outline it is, became jagged and rough and broken. If there is a loss in sculptural monumentality, there is a great gain in expressiveness: the power is continuous, a given, a constant. Working in the deliberate, demanding medium of fresco meant that Orozco had to plan the work in great a priori detail. Fresco painting does not allow for the spontaneous, the off-hand, the impromptu; one must perforce plan for every square inch of space, of wall, that one means to cover with painted designs. A veritable mass of masterly Orozco drawings is the resulting benefice of that necessity. The drawings delineate in their probing and unyielding honesty the web of human diversity, the ever-returning cycle of human history; the struggles, the aspirations, the debacles, the betrayals, the renewals, the rebirths, the losses, the resuscitations, the defeats, the deaths; the ongoing human outreach for equity, for probity, the persistent, anguished human desire for peace, for grace, for dignity. Sergei Eisenstein called Orozco "The Prometheus of Mexican painting", and how apt and accurate that epithet is. For Orozco is promethean in the surging immensity of his achievement; he is promethean in his consistency, his continuous growth and his rootedness in the human condition. Orozco is promethean in the demi-urge of his encompassing power.

Tino da Camaino

A long autobiographical intrusion into the supposed impersonalisms of
these writings: all of these artists have struck responsively at my
artistic consciousness; some directly so, with hammer-throws to the
heart, others have piqued my notice, and aroused my curiosities anent
their circumstance, how they and their times meshed or proved
mutually incohesive, and yet others alerted me to unthought-of
possibilities; and finally, those who performed the crucial rôles of
model and praxis, teaching and leading, the masters one clasps to
one's heart. Such a one is Tino da Camaino. A spring morning in 1951
which began deliberately and ended haphazardly became the crucial
moment in my "Wanderjahr"; on that memorable spring morning I
boarded the 6 a.m. bus from Florence to Pisa. That entire springtime
was spent in the golden, if rather rainy purlieus of Florence, sating my
eyes and my intelligence at the Bargello, the churches, the Uffizi and
everywhere else: I was enrolled as a scholar at the Accademia di Belle
Arte under the high auspices of the GI Bill of Rights. I had intended
to go to Siena, city of dulcet painting and strong sculpture, but missed
by a moment or two the only early morning bus. Determined to give
fulfillment to my travel set, and travel somewhere, to my surprised
and very sleepy self I boarded the bus bound for Pisa. Pisa was
despised by the ignorant cognoscenti as Siena was touted: Pisa, the
dread city of purest tourism, of ridiculously corny leaning towers, the
suspect object of philistinic veneration. My ignorance was boundless.
Shall I ever forget that first sight, in full spring sunshine, of the Pisan
Cathedral, Baptistry, and the Campanile? A stony triad of consummate
grace and felicity, starkly and uninterruptedly visible in their
containing greensward; a superb vision of informing relatedness, of
divine proportion; an amazing disposition of great masses of diverse
shape, size and function which form a stony harmony of exquisite
strength. But those beautiful marmorean behemoths, lambent in their
green context, were the least of the Pisan wonders of that miraculous
day. For many years I had foundered in my attempts to make
sculptures; at the onset and for a remarkably long time, I was an inept
fumbler, a tyro (taking but small comfort and solace from the
indisputable fact that sculptural prodigies are an unknown

Pisanello. we. 1960.

31

phenomenon). Complicating the muddy ineptitude further was my infantile attempt to communicate specific political ideas in three-dimensionality. The history of my oafish and awkward strivings has – thank God – been told elsewhere. It led to my making woodcuts, which is the only favor of that harrowing experience. Much of 1950 had been spent at Paris, where at the Louvre I discovered Sumerian sculpture and saw that miracle of contained energy, the Hera of Samos. Those sculptures taught me the fundamental laws of monumentality. Circled about one of the tiers of the Pisan Baptistry is set a series of heroic and monumental sculptures of saints and prophets by the great Giovanni Pisano. I was stunned by the force of those carvings, their primacy, power and their hulking, brooding expressiveness; I was profoundly moved by those innovative works, especially the ones I could observe and examine at closer range, which had been moved, for preservation's sake, to the confines of the Museo Nazionale. I must admit that I emulated Galileo and countless other climbers to the askew top of that ridiculously marvelous, wedding-cake tower. Of the cathedral and its fabled bronze doors, I shall say naught, nor more than note the famous Campo Santo whose lead roof seams were disastrously set afire by World War Two incendiary bombs, causing the molten lead to run down the walls and destroying everything thereon; the salvaged and massively restored Orcagna mural is now hung, still quite glorious, at the Museo Nazionale at Pisa. At that museum is also housed the sculptural group that rehearsed, reinforced and enlarged the lessons taught by the diorites and basalts of Sumer. I casually and ignorantly walked into the museum and saw for the first time the extraordinary sculptural memorial to Arrigo VIII. Sitting cross-legged, stiffly and kingly upright, the memorialized monarch is surrounded by a group of memorable servitors. In 1970 I wrote about "Harry VIII and His Courtiers": "The qualities of lyric power and monumentality here reappeared in modern sculpture. The courtiers stand variously about the king, forming with him a vivid but silent harmony, stiff and intense, long-robed, they unexpectedly turn ever so slightly, or lift back a head, or lean, or bend imperceptibly; these sudden movements remind one of how a motionless bird abruptly cocks its head. Their

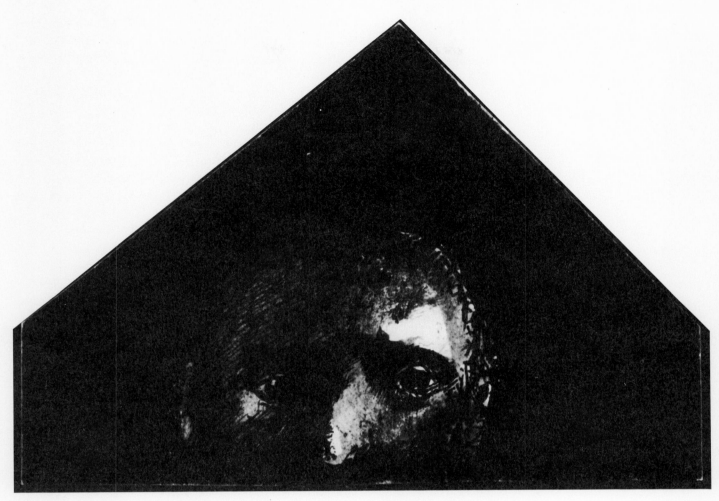

Tino da Camaino. drawing. 1986.

stark frontality precludes the probability of movement, but so subtly is the work wrought, we delight in the unexpected gesture. They stand thus, seemingly straining in homage to their fiercely uptight immobile king. All of Tino's figures, men, women, children, putti, angels, have great round cheeks, as do his courtiers in Pisa, which tend to make the courtiers non-specific, to have them imply all courtiers everywhere: the quality of generalising found in all monumental sculpture. The contained silhouette, the stony fluidity, the felicitous power make the courtiers kin to Lagash, to the Pharaohs, to the Hera of Samos. I spent that day absorbing the marrow of those sculptures, learning the rhythms that moved from figure to figure, finding in their tilts and bows and leanings the adumbrations of style, and in their tonality the sounds of a voice to which I was attuned." Fifteen years later I look back to Tino as capping the crucial and the primary enlightenment, that taught me the fundamental qualities of sculpture. Those standing courtiers, attending Arrigo, have a contained outline, very like the great Sumerian carving that I had seen and apprehended at the British Museum and at the Louvre; Tino softens the rigidities, unbends the stiffnesses, enlivens the silhouette, and provided for my greedy eyes the first demonstration of possible variations of that sculpture-sustaining envelope of forms. Those courtiers are formally very like Han and early Tang dynasty ceramic sculptures; the slight, sudden, contained movement, a swelling here and a drape barely rustling there, the body subtly curved, an arm half-lifted: of the movements, one can perhaps say that they are just begun. Of Tino's other works I only note his "Caritas" at the Bardini Collection, Florence. The great mother-figure, round-faced and abundant of form, feeds her two symbolic full-cheeked babies. The Trecento is here being ventilated with a humanizing wind. It is in the Circle of Arnolfo di Cambio that Tino revolves, but vested in Tino are those particularities of subtle power that spoke so emphatically to my artistic need.

34

Mantegna. etching. 1952.

Andrea Mantegna

Three of the greatest paintings of corpses are by Mantegna, Holbein and Rembrandt: all three were intent on painting a corpse; Mantegna and Holbein used the ready device of a depiction of Christ; Rembrandt used a doctor's "anatomy". Holbein's great mortuarial figure disposed on a cold marble slab, vibrating yet with its just lost liveliness, lies beyond our interest in this Mantegnaesque context, as its conception has naught to do with Mantua in the late fifteenth century; whereas Rembrandt's "Anatomy Lesson of Dr Deyman" has its central figure directly and entirely depending from Mantegna's "Dead Christ". Rembrandt's anatomized corpse is foreshortened in precisely Mantegna's way. Dr Deyman stands or sits directly behind the exposed skull of his dead criminal, the cortex flowing out of it like a mass of abundant blond hair. The young courtier-like attendant to Dr Deyman's right is elegantly holding what appears to be a bowl; what he holds is the top of the corpse's skull. Rembrandt forces our enchanted gaze beyond the tips of the toes, directly into a vast thoracic cavity, driving us through and beyond that excavated chest into the dead face and opened and flowing head. Rembrandt was directly tutored in this longest viewpoint and extravagant positioning by Andrea Mantegna, an artist he profoundly admired. Rembrandt owned several Mantegna drawings and many of his original and beautiful engravings; indeed, Rembrandt made a copy of Mantegna's drawing of "The Calumny of Appelles". Rembrandt might have learned the audacious Mantegnaesque foreshortening from a number of prints heavily influenced by it; for instance, Orazio Baglione etched a dead Christ seen in Mantegna's foreshortening, and drawings after the painting may well have circulated from studio to studio, especially finding their way to Rembrandt's, who collected in an uncontrollable frenzy. One is stunned at first viewing Mantegna's "Dead Christ"; it hangs slightly lower than eye-level at the Brera in Milan: one looks downwards into the compassionately insistent, compelling and commanding deadness of Christ. The forms are tesserae-like in their obdurate solidity, their grey-greenness rendering them marmorial and granitic. Are the looking-on presences of the Virgin and St John an afterthought, an effort on Mantegna's part to lift what is palpably an intellectual enterprise in delineating the nude male figure in extreme foreshortening? But often the most hide-bound exercises carry an unintended meaning, a non-deliberate penetration of reality, an unlooked-for substance that transforms the work; and when the artist is a titan, the work can achieve a transubstantiation, forging out of experiment and exercise, works that convincingly move us. Thus, I think that Mantegna's "Dead Christ" betrays his primary intention, and although we marvel at Mantegna's ingenious perspective, the work vests into our consciousnesses as a painting probing human tragedy, grief, and the extreme disharmonies of dolor. Mantegna requires no panegyrical odes, no vindicative texts and no celebratory sanctions – he is a world master, a prime mover of the Italian Renaissance, whose influence radiated from his North Italian site to every part of cultured Europe, reaching into seventeenth-century Holland and affecting Rembrandt. Mantegna was a choleric and saturnine man, in temperament excitable, aggressive, explosive but not in the carousing, murdering class of Caravaggio: Mantegna was parsimonious, greedy, argumentative; he nagged his patrons and he was abrasive in virtually all of his dealings. He built a fine house undistinguished except for a surprising octagonal courtyard of considerable size. He was an intense and knowledgeable collector of antique objects. His painting style is three-dimensional, infused with his knowledge of antique sculpture: his work is compounded out of fully realized big forms, brilliantly hued color, stunning and unerring draughtsmanship, great knowledge of classical and religious iconography and symbolism, and the divine gift to compose and to orchestrate these elements into paintings of compelling passion and power. Isabella D'Este, the proud and ferocious patron and ardent collector, lusted after an antique portrait bust of Faustina in Mantegna's collection; he beat back her attempts to cajole it from him. She did get it, however, when he was old and counted himself penurious; it has survived, that bust of Faustina, and one wonders at Isabella's passion for it, doubtless because it was Mantegna's. Perhaps I have drawn too dark a portrait of Andrea Mantegna; he burned with too hot an incarnadine puissance, was consumed with the desire to refine the forms of his paintings, to extend the edges of his craft, to deepen his perceptions, to enlarge the meanings and dimensions of his art.

Mantegna. we. 1960.

De Barbari. we. 1960.

Jacopo de Barbari

Jacopo de Barbari, an enigmatic artist, art historically, worked for the
Saxons at various ducal and princely courts, beginning in 1500; he was
at Wurtenburg in 1505, was a colleague there of Lucas Cranach; in
1510 he was even named Valet de chambre et peintre attaché à la
princesse Margaret of Austria, and worked with Gossaert for Philip of
Burgundy who called them, "nostrae aetatis Zeuxim et Alpellera": and
who commissioned them to decorate his new residence, the castle of
Lonburg. Perhaps of greater importance was his acquaintance with
Dürer, whom he met in Venice in 1494/5; Dürer writes of de Barbari
on three occasions and tried to buy a de Barbari sketchbook from
Margaret, Regent of the Netherlands, when he visited Malines.
Remarkable how certain figures invented by de Barbari reappear in
various northern artists' work; the mighty Dürer felt his influence and
used a de Barbari design for his engraved figure of Apollo. De Barbari
had an unusually delicate touch in his engravings, especially when
compared to the power-driven burin of Mantegna, the crude delights
of Zoan Andrea, the lyric radiances of Christofano Robetta: his dulcet
subtleties are surprising in the refractory medium of engraving in
copper. De Barbari was a deep participant in the rediscovery or
exploitation of ancient Greece and Rome: among his relatively small
engraved oeuvre can be counted two of "Sacrifice to Priapus", an
"Apollo and Diana" and "Mars and Venus", a "Triton and Nereid"
and a rather Germanic duo called "Victory and Glory", a "Pegasus"
and others. De Barbari's figures are unnaturally tall and languidly
sinuous; they seem lost in a meditative tristesse. De Barbari is, as
Wurzbach has noted, a fusion of Venetian individuality, Flemish and
German technique, Antique idealism and Nordic realism. A true son
of Mercury, de Barbari engraved the caduceus into virtually each of his
prints, never his name; he was long known as the "Master of the
Caduceus". Two works of de Barbari have particularly interested me:
the great woodcut map of Venice, enormously large; in it de Barbari
spreads Venice before us in its convoluted, anfractuous complexity, its
eight encircling winds blowing furiously, ships thrusting at the big
island like a horde of overturned black beetles; a gigantic, heaven-
gazing trident-holding Neptune sits astride a dolphin guarding the

mouth of the lagoon. Mercury fills up the sky directly above Neptune grasping a magnificent Mercurial wand, looking down with benevolent wonder at the most artistic and most fanciful of cities. The map is a marvel of clarity, brilliance in design, and cut with an exacting finesse. One painting, long considered as by de Barbari, but in the current de-attributing vogue, doubted, has riveted my attention. It is a portrait of Fra Luca Pacioli in Franciscan habit, and of the young Duke Guidobaldo of Urbino to whom Pacioli dedicated his "Summa de Arithmetica" published in 1495; to Pacioli's right suspended on a fine thread is a crystal polyhedron magical in its multidimensionality; we perceive its front and back at once, the object's facets absorbing and reflecting light; a luminous landscape is seen reflected in one of the polished surfaces as though seen through an unknown window. Fra Luca points to a slate inscribed with an equilateral triangle within a circle, and indicates a book with his other hand. The book, probably a Euclid that he edited, lies open on a carpeted table, its edges inscribed "LIR.LVC.BVR.", the letters in abbreviation for "Liber Reverendi Luc Burgensis". This monumentally serious portrait is of Luca Pacioli of Borgo San Sepulchro, the friend in childhood and later of Piero della Francesca, with whom he explored the intricate geometrics and golden vexations of perspective, sections and proportion. It is generally agreed that Luca Pacioli commissioned the designs for his crucial book "De Divine Proportione" (Venice, 1509) from Leonardo. This scientific portrait is wonderful for the quality of magic that pervades it, despite the divers exacting instruments and the sharp-angled hedrons that litter it and the various icons of knowledge. The books open and closed that lie on the table do not contest the sense of phantom unreality: that glowing, fulgent, mysterious, immense crystal looming like a third character in the painting, and opposed to all of this the sudden real personification of Fra Luca and his patron: like a premature Lorenzo Lotto, Jacopo de Barbari has infused these portraits with the psychological qualities of life.

Alfonso da Tomaso Ruspagiari

Unfailingly, mingled sensations of delight and astonishment, perhaps
even of astounded pleasure, flare up within me whenever I happen
upon a critic condemning a virtue in a work as a fault. It is typically a
quality of particular excellence or a superbly achieved part that sparks
the critic's fatuity. It is the usage of these stuffed cognoscenti that they

41

abhor the atypical and the ruffling; they have a mad desire for the undisturbed, the placid (I will not say flaccid), the unruffled, the standard, the expected: they unfailingly traduce anything that distances itself from their divine norms. They particularly abhor excess. (Witness Blake's apothegms in *The Marriage of Heaven and Hell*, "The road of excess leads to the palace of wisdom" and "Exuberance is Beauty.") The great Emilian sixteenth-century medalist Alfonso da Tomaso Ruspagiari has been the victim of these later Victorian, and alas still current, critical lapses and crudities. Ruspagiari has never had an equal in low relief modeling; one is startled into gaping wonder at the marvelous subtleties of Ruspagiari's low relief modeling. That he is the consummate master of the lowest relief is universally admitted. But Ruspagiari had a wanton love of drapery. His fair and beautiful women seemed breathed onto the tiny circumferences of his bronze-cast medals. The molten surfaces of these medals are suffused with an unimaginable delicacy, but not wanting in strength or purpose; indeed, these works of art are not irrelevant flippancies. They are evocative of one of the sixteenth century's many moods. Ruspagiari is a Mannerist. His medals are indubitably both erotic and neurotic, but subtly so. He did take endless delight in draperies. His men and his women both are swaddled in draperies of an evanescent lightness; the gently twisting bodies, the sudden lifting heads, or the slightly lifting arms are encased in small clouds of draped linens and cottons. And it is in that excess of drapery that Ruspagiari arouses the ire of the experts. It is its rapturous, excessive quality that is detested. G. F. Hill in his book *Portrait Models of Italian Artists of the Renaissance* (London, 1912) writes: "He delights in showing his virtuosity in the treatment of fine and much-folded drapery, rather hung about the body than worn; the ladies whom he represents are all 'drest about the head . . . with embroyderies, frizelings, and carcanets of pearle' (Montaigne); the busts are supported on fantastic brackets, and the arms truncated as if they were carved in stone. These affectations are hardly compensated by the extreme delicacy of his modelling in low relief." How inept that savant was to carp at the essence of Ruspagiari's genius. Ruspagiari, given the nature of court life in Mannerist times, invests his medals with cytherean phantasies, his medals invoke the world of the courtly masque, of innuendo, of artificiality, of gossip and of dolce far niente.

Ruspagiari. drawing. 1980.

If his wondrously overlapping drapes cannot be called imbricated, they do indeed flow from one into another with near imperceptibility, and with an easy felicity. The medals have an extravagant lyricism and are amongst the most beautiful medals of the Renaissance, the prime time of medal making. Very little is known about his life. We do not control, either through indifference or with deliberation, our posterities. We know this odd bit of Ruspagiari's history. He had four daughters; their names and dates of birth are: Filarida Anna, 12 March 1541, Dalia Anna, 31 May 1556, Celia, 1 February 1559 and Isabella (date not known). He was "descended from one of the patrician families of his native city (Reggio d'Emilia) and was very well connected" (Forer). "Contemporary documents show that he held a prominent position in the council of Reggio, and that he was several times deputed to superintend public works" (Forer). Modeling in relief sits haphazardly and rather precariously between sculpture and painting, wanting their great strengths. Although, if worked boldly, three-dimensionality can be assertively achieved, in the hands of its greatest practitioners mystifying effects of volume were realized by the controls of the gentlest of swellings and the mildest of depressions. The demands put on line increases in direct relationship to the lowness of the relief; the line plays a crucial rôle in the attainment of volumetric effects, in the expression of great roundness using the shallowest of means. There is a quality about Ruspagiari's medals that for the dire want of another word I shall call "sfumato", in the way the forms melt into one another. His edges tend to be at the delineative perimeters of his forms, as in a Piazzetta drawing, allowing the interior to exist in the subtlest subsumption of forms by other forms. It sounds rather buttery and weak, but it isn't, for Ruspagiari controls these means with the tightest probity in form and delineation. The further restriction which the small compass of the medal imposes requires the sculptor a degree of virtuosity in modeling that is beyond one's ready understanding. There exists a flood of medals, beginning in the late Quattrocento; the medium became a political and humanistic toy and achieved vast popularity. Ruspagiari stands alone in style, manner and force; there were a few, rather excellent Emilian imitators; they merely confirm Ruspagiari's originality, poetic force and genius.

Stefano Della Bella

The inevitable coupling of Jacques Callot and Della Bella is understandable. Neither painted or made sculpture, but drew and etched, consummately, continually and fervently: their oeuvre is immense. I have etched their portraits. Although Callot must be deemed the greater artist, his "Balli di Sfesannia", "Disasters of War", "Nobility of Lorraine", "Gobbi" and "Capriccio" are only occasionally matched by della Bella. They are both decidedly great, and in the end Stefano Della Bella is clasped to one's sensibilities with greater avidity and affection. It is that slashing cavalier stroke which, although present in Callot, has a wild swashbuckling demeanor in Della Bella, that is captivating and endearing; especially when he deploys that devastating skill in subjects that are dear to my heart. He was much preoccupied with representations of death. A large and dramatic print has death astride a skeleton horse, insanely dashing across a field where the detritus of carnage litters the ground. In a suite of five prints called "The Five Deaths", but to which I have lent the Victorian title, "Death's Doings", death sardonically helps an old man into his grave, and in a depiction of the plague, death kidnaps forever a baby, thrusting it violently over its bony shoulder and runs off with it. In another, death drives his steed directly at us, a masterstroke of perspective and brilliant drawing. Della Bella had a flair for ornament and variously exercised it: he etched a set of friezes, funerary and bizarre, using death as the central decorative element in the compositions. The prints are brilliant, the skulls and skeletal parts all mingled with ribands and garlands, and in a wonderful series of fanciful vases, death-heads often form the body of the vases. There is in Della Bella at his best and perceptible in the freshest impressions of his engravings, qualities of direct spontaneity, a certainty and a surity that vivifies and enlivens the work. He was apparently interested in everything as his numerous and various prints testify.

Della Bella or Callot. we. 1958.

45

Wenceslas Hollar

Wenceslas Hollar was a tireless etcher. Parthy lists well over two thousand prints in his oeuvre. We have glimpses of him in Aubrey and Evelyn; he was a poor manager of monies for he is often in financial distress, a remarkable state for a person of Hollar's industry and enterprise. He seems to have been continuously employed by Lord Arundel, engraving his numerous paintings and drawings, his marbles, his seats and even his insects. Arundel took Hollar along as "artiste en voyage" when he made a trip down the Rhine and further traveling to North Africa, Hollar drawing and later etching everything that was visible, especially the landscape and town views. He was endlessly employed by the publishers, and in appreciative demand by divers celebrated antiquarians, Dugdale and Ashmole to name two of widest renown. We see his etchings through the endless pages of *Monasticum Anglicorum*, and in *The Antiquities of Warwickshire* and many another county history. He magnificently portrays the ancient Gothic-space-filled old cathedral in *The History of St Paul's* and in *The History of the Garter* costume, badges and jewels flash in vivid renditions. Amongst his seemingly endless productions are the mysterious etchings for Benlowe's *Theophilia* and the enchanting ones in quite large size for a beautiful edition of Aesop. Hollar produced two ravishing sets of female costume, the *Theatrum Mulierum* and the *Laus Venerae* in which the women of the world are arrayed and convincingly displayed in the particularities of their countries' dress. Hollar's needle was capable of finesses of the greatest delicacy, as in what must be counted among his capital achievements, the four wondrous etchings of women and bouquets representing the four seasons, original works by Hollar, instantly recognizable as such and unforgettable for their range of tonality, their subtlety and their finish in representing the seasons in gesture, in costume and in floral variety. It is inevitable that, in so prodigious a production and often in such hackneyed byways, much that Hollar etched is soulless and mechanical and boring. The views of Windsor Castle in *The History of the Garter*, seen from various compass vantage points, are unexpected and surprising in an otherwise mostly dull book. The quality of impression is often crucial in Hollar; the moths and butterflies are glorious in rich impressions, and lose their magical, one might say palpitating, vivacity in dull impressions, especially the deep necessary,

Hollar. drawing. 1987.

enlivening blackness in the curled caterpillar. In addition to the etchings of the "Four Seasons" and the great print of "Antwerp Cathedral", Hollar is famous for his etchings of muffs. Inevitably erotic, these beautiful fur muffs are a kind of public pubicity, and they are so darkly evocative and lustrous in texture that they stand in isolation within Hollar's work and the graphic arts of his time and place. Our perception and our visual knowledge of seventeenth-century England would be vastly impoverished if we were deprived of Hollar's titanic production.

Henry Fuseli

> The only Man that e'er I knew
> Who did not make me almost spew
> Was Fuseli; he was both Turk and Jew –
> And so, dear Christian Friends, how do ye do?   Blake

To have won that impish doggerel from Blake, who tended to use the form for the general excoriation of his enemies, lifts Fuseli to a very high pedestal. Blake cannot contain his praise for Fuseli, as witness this encomium: "Such an artist as Fuseli is invulnerable, he needs not my defence; but I should be ashamed not to set my hand and shoulder and whole strength against those wretches who, under the pretence of criticism, use the dagger and the poison." In the end Fuseli philosophically abandoned Blake to mysticism and his invented mythologies, but they remained friends, and the affectionate candor of Fuseli's aside, "Blake is damned good to steal from," resonates through Time's narrowest corridor. I do not know why this short expatiatory piece on Henry Fuseli should be so larded with praiseworthy if supernumerary quotations. Sir Thomas Lawrence, who was a great connoisseur and a fair painter, noted at the death of Fuseli, "We have just sustained the loss of kindred [Michelangelo] genius, if not greater, in the original and lofty conceptions of Mr Fuseli. In poetic invention it is not too much to say he has no equal since the Fifteenth or Sixteenth centuries, and if his drawings and proportions were mannered and sometimes carried to excess, still it was exaggeration of the grandeur of antique form and not – as in many – enlargement of the mean and ordinary in nature." And there is Benjamin Robert Haydon, the friend and portrayer of Keats and the author of a splendid autobiography which far exceeds in quality any of his painted works, in which he was bedevilled by visions of gigantic "History" pictures, which his puerile talents would not permit him to achieve. He killed himself on 22 June 1846. Haydon ceaselessly arranged columns of friends and enemies on the issue of the Elgin Marbles, whose savior he was, and who was bewitched and bemused and made mad, perhaps simply madder, by their near universal neglect. Haydon did not perceive Fuseli as fully enough supporting

Fuseli. lithograph. 1969.

the marmorean struggle and yet he wrote of Fuseli, "Fuseli was undoubtedly the greatest genius of that age. His Milton Gallery showed a range and imagination equal to the poet; . . . " In that context and from that muddled artist, remarkable praise indeed. I will touch on only one aspect of Fuseli's accomplishment; leaving unnoticed his amazing paintings to Shakespeare and Milton, his single most famous work, "The Nightmare", and significant related works. Fuseli observed with that special prescient gift that some artists possess, "One of the most unexplored regions of art are dreams." Fuseli was reared and trained to be a Lutheran pastor, and he was deeply learnéd in Greek and Roman literature and history, translated and published divers works while still young, and was (a family tradition) an accomplished entomologist. "There are listed twenty-three different works on entomology in his effects' sale catalogue, including Moses Harris's beautiful 'Aurelian, or the Natural History of English Insects, namely Moths and Butterflies', as well as a collection of no less than two hundred drawings, mostly of North American insects by a Georgian artist, J. Abbot." Fuseli was in stature very small, in personality vexatious, volatile, and he was immensely learnéd; in addition to Greek and Latin, he knew Hebrew, German (his native tongue, he was born at Zurich), French, Italian, English of course, and a sufficiency of Dutch. He had a famous platonic affair with Mary Wollstonecraft, until, it was said, his wife "put a stop to it". That Fuseli was also a great artist is wondrous. He said, "I do not wish to build a stage, but to erect a pyramid." It is Fuseli's drawings of women that haunt my memory. Haydon said of them, ". . . his women are all strumpets, . . ." and Ruthven Todd observes in his imaginative book, *Tracks in the Snow*, "Those drawings show women engaged in ordinary tasks, dressing for a ball or embroidering a scarf, or merely standing and waiting; yet, into these commonplace scenes, Fuseli has managed to infuse something of the pure clarity of a dream . . . all the women have immense or elaborate coiffures (which appear only in these and in his obscene drawings), and even the placing of a cup upon a table seems to have some terrible hidden significance." And again, "His tall, fantastic women clad in parodies of the long, clinging dresses of the period are, as Haydon suggests, procuresses and whores, haggling and tempting, . . . and all their everyday and

50

trivial actions have become charged with the significance of magical rites; the terrible and the sublime pale into insignificance besides these drawings where the domestic scene enters the realm of the dream." Fuseli often used his wife as model for these drawings of courtesans, whose brightness of costume gleams against the deep umbrage of the rooms and against the chimney-pieces against which they often lounge. It is those long, white evocative gowns enclosing the long, suave, lissome, sinuous, lascivious women that live on in one's consciousness. I do not mean those truly pornographic drawings by Fuseli, bits of which have tantalizingly been reproduced here and there and finally fully reproduced in the post-war Danish aura of freer, looser sexual expressiveness; those drawings are adventurous, exploring all aspects of sexual reality and phantasy. The drawings which gleam vividly in my memory are far more beautiful, expressive and haunting. They are of harlots, one presumes, usually in twos, unoccupied, standing about, or devilishly, invitingly perched on sofas, and in other and fanciful positions, not languorous but intensely alert, as in that quite incredible drawing of two women looking out of a window, that is, they are precariously bending, far out of the window, looking upwards, starkly visible against the very dark interior. The women have enormous coiffures, hair piled up in obsessive abundance. Fuseli's brilliance of draughtsmanship reinforces his uncanny capacity to render the unlikely as real, to make believable and palpable the unnaturalness of the position of ungainly excessive bending-out, the bizarreness of the viewpoint, that looking high-up, the artificiality of gesture, the additional compounding caused by one of the women toying with a rope and pulley, all of these directly and succinctly relate to Sturm und Drang; Fuseli was proto-Romantic, a disciple of Bodmer. His work is replete with notions of the horrific, the extreme, the bardic (he invented the ur-image of the Bard, high on a cliff-edge, declaiming Macphersonian epic lines). The frantic, exuberant early Romantic themes resonate distinctly, clearly and voluminously in Fuseli's drawings. I give you three titles of drawings: "A Courtesan with Naked Breast, Sitting in front of a Fire, Holding a Switch; behind her to the left a Small Crouching Fairy"; another, "Callipyga, a Woman with her Shirt Lifted Standing before a Dressing Table with Phallic Supports", and another, "Half-length Figure of a

Courtesan with Feathers, a Bow and a Veil in her Hair". But these drawings of prostitutes (?) have mellifluous mellowness trapped within their strangeness; some are entirely odd, as the two drawings of a bare-breasted high-coiffed woman approaching the Laocoön, and some are aggressively and splendidly sexual; for instance the "Three Women with Baskets Descending a Staircase" is full of Fuselian twists and turns (Fuseli owned a considerable number of Mannerist prints) and the seeming inevitable presence of a pointing woman; the women descend the stairs, sharply turning from shade to light, perhaps a moment out of an emergent Gothic novel. Typically, with the many women in the many drawings seen to sit or stand expectantly, one cannot help but speculate what these women are up to. Do they participate in that long tradition of depicted idle but oppressed women, lounging about in tepidariums, or harems, or bordellos, waiting to be called? These courtesans of Fuseli have naught in common with the luscious, over-heated eroticism of later Romanticism, nor with the cooler eroticism of Titian's "Venuses" or Cranach's "Dianas". Fuseli has been diagnosed, considerably after the fact, a hair-fetishist; and this and other likely features of his work have been fruitlessly, I think, subjected to Freudian analysis within the context of art history. Just as confusion is the end of all attempts to make certain attributions among the drawings of Adam Elsheimer and Count H. Goudt, so a similar if smaller but intriguing problem exists among several drawings of Fuseli and John Brown, the Edinburgh artist who died of consumption at age thirty-five. In his very best drawings of Roman women ("Three Roman Ladies", "A Roman Lady with a Duenna"), Brown veered very close to the masterly qualities of Fuseli. He was powerfully influenced by Fuseli. Recent scholarship has suggested that Fuseli was in turn touched by Brown. A felicitous instance of that fructifying dialectic of influence doubling back on itself; it is a kind of rearticulation, a rediscovery of source; an aged Fuseli reinspired by his own vision seen anew in a younger artist.

Allan. drawing. 1986.

Anne Allan

While painstakingly studying and surveying Johannes Teyler's ''Opus Typochromaticum'' at the British Museum, I noticed the faintest marginal notations, in a fine but firm hand, running throughout the book. Determined to snatch every mystery from Teyler's epochal and innovative work I troubled to decipher and to copy those faded rubrics. Teyler invented a method of printing, from an etched or engraved plate, many colors, with one pass through the copperplate press. This technique is now universally called printing "à la poupée". The poupée is a small stump made of cloth, which is used as a dabber for applying the different color; a different poupée for each color. If the plate is carefully wiped, with sharp attentiveness in the matter of directional wiping, a complexity of numerous adjacent colors can be achieved. Teyler was extraordinarily skillful in fixing with great clarity a multitude of colors; which led Humbert in 1752 to name his method "marquetterie".

Johannes Teyler was born at Nijmegen in 1648 and was later professor of Philosophy and Mathematics there. He traveled, taught at the Brandenburgian court, and was in Rome, where he became a member of the "Bentvugheuls". He died soon after 1697. The "Opus Typochromaticum" is a collection of proofs, made by Teyler, using his own etchings and engravings and any other copperplates he could find. The subjects of these beautiful colorprints are wonderfully various, ranging from landscapes in Italy and Holland, architectural subjects and flowerpieces. It is a rich and magnificent work. At the very end of the mammoth Typochromaticum I discoverd in that telltale hand the name Anne Pillement. The notes were written by the mysterious Anne Allan. It had long been assumed that Anne Allan and Jean-Baptiste Pillement had been married; here at last was proof. Anne Allan had etched forty-five plates after drawings by Pillement of fanciful chinoiseries; pellucid, muted and subtle. They have a dazzling burnished clarity: these unique colored prints are true to Pillement's drawing, lending a newer enhancement to the entities of chinoiserie. These fairyland phantasies are organized into nine sets, with engraved titlepieces, which read, "Nouvelle suite de Cahiers arabesques chinois a l'usage des dessineteurs et des peintres, inv. et des. par Jean Pillement, gravés par Anne Allan" or "Nouvelle suite de Fleurs idéals a l'usage des dessineteurs et des peintres inv. et des. par Jean Pillement, gravé par Anne Allan. No. 5." As Guilmard dryly notes, "charmants motifs imprimés en couleur." I laboriously transcribed the copious notes, modernized and edited them into sequential readability, and present them here for the first time. It constitutes a veritable Anne Allan redivivus. "Like all the gifted English, I was born into the North, in Yorkshire at Heptonstall, a small but industrious village. Demonstrating an early and a quick capacity for drawing and colouring and not readily dissuaded by the deluge of argument that spilled about me, attempting to allay my artistic strivings, accompanied by all the inevitable cries of unnaturalness, unsuitability, wanton disregard of decency, etc., my great aunt Hannah Allan suggested that I should unsex myself, if I pursued this ill-tempered, hysterical headstrong course, which served to spur me on. Familial and local difficulties mounted as my determination increased and as I sought professional training. The obdurance of my family's opposition did not for a moment abate, the situation at home grew increasingly insupportable, and on the day after my sixteenth birthday, summoning resolve and strengths, I left my unsympathetic home, without parental blessing and in penury and thus began for me the strain of survival amongst strangers in an alien world and remaining chaste as I moved along the broad highways towards the South. Making my inept and inexperienced way to Manchester, a chance stagecoach meeting led to a post as drawing teacher to the daughters of an aristocratic Mancunian family. The teaching tasks allowed me considerable time in which to push on with my studies in painting and drawing. I was distressed to discover that painting in oils was pertinently inimical to my talents, my proclivity and my strength was in drawing and in engraving which is necessarily subsidiary to and consequent of drawing. Restless in Manchester and brimful of anxiety to be at the boiling centre of the country's artistic life, I made my way to London. London was a blur of bewilderment; its immensities gave me the staggers; its endless moving columns of people and carriages, the mansions and the palaces, the fetid back alleys, the stagnant pools, the stews and the huge, stout, forbidding, excluding houses and all wreathed in fog, a terrifying eructation of a place, but my Mancunian masters had given me several letters of introduction: they proved salvatory in the colossal and foreign realities of London. One introduction led inevitably to another, and as my vectoring was toward the professional artists, I found myself inevitably drawn to those engravers in stipple and the crayon manner specifically but moving in artistic circles generally. Odd to note and perhaps prelusive to my future undertakings, I fell in with chiefly foreign masters, resident in London during the 1780s. Noteworthy in their help to me were the sets of brothers, Georg Sigmund and Johann Gottlieb Facius, and Heinrich and Peter Sintzenich. I became, under their tutelages, very proficient in divers etching and engraving techniques. The great stroke of good fortune anent my career was a chance meeting at Romney's studio with the artist Maria Cosway. We became fast and true friends and our small, intimate and sentimental circle included her husband Richard, the famous miniature painter, and Maria's great and special friend the American gallant Thomas Jefferson and John Condé, the Fleming who engraved her paintings and her drawings into objects of immense fame and popularity. One day while taking tea with Maria in the larger drawing room in the house at Bryanston Square, she asked me whether I had ever seen her great Johannes Teyler book. Can you conceive my delight and amazement as I regarded Teyler's incredible blazing variety? The virtuosity involved in printing so many colours from a single copper amazed me and I near instantaneously determined that Teyler would prove my ultimate master. He being long dead, the great book itself became my purest model, my devotional praxis, the glowing paradigm toward which I aspired. How the Opus Typochromaticum came into Maria's hands, entails the travels of an indifferent Dutch etcher, who in the throes of a passion for Maria, brought it to her, one day, for a gift. Maria's interest in Teyler's work was minimal, tending to regard technical matters as not central to her concern, considering it a matter for the attention of her engravers who were entirely preoccupied with aquatint and the reproduction of tonality. I could not get enough of Teyler and his enormous opus. I presented myself daily at Bryanston Sq. asking to see Maria. I made a veritable pest of myself. Maria was quite amused by the overwhelming impact Teyler's single-plated clarion of colour had on me, but my incessant calling at her house (I was living relatively close-by at Lisson Grove, near Haydon) began to interfere with her amorous liaison with Jefferson, Richard being very often away painting miniature portraits of the English nobility and the very rich. To be rid of the plague of my visiting and staying and sitting and studying, and to prevent my becoming a situate fixture in her house, Maria resorted to the extreme measure of heaving the Typochromaticum into my arms, announcing that the deucéd book

56

Allan. drawing. 1986.

was now my property and would I please leave her in peace. Overcome and in a near uncontrollable state, I struggled to my rooms, barely able to bear the heavy treasure. The gift was to me of incalculable worth. I ceased my daily visits to Maria's house and threw myself into the total mastery of Teyler's book. In what I counted as a quick passage of time, I found I could imitate Teyler's most complex printing of colour. I added several devices of my own inventing, as viz. the adding of a second plate allowing a doubling of the numbers of colours. Never having had the gifts of invention highly developed, and with my incapacity to paint in oils, my artistic intentions were indubitably reproductive in nature, but before setting-up as a reproductive engraver I thought a salutary trip to the continent to be in order. I removed myself to Paris, replete with masses of trial and experimental proofs: if you think that the great weight and size obviated the hauling along of the 'Opus Typochromaticum', then I have not sufficiently impressed upon you its crucial importance in my artistic consciousness. However difficult, it accompanied me. The Paris of the 1790s was the Paris of Jaminet and of Dubucourt, of Le Blonc and of Gautier D'Agoty. The frenzy of colour printing was in the air and I plunged into the delirium of the Rue St. Jacques. The intaglio printing shops along that fabled street were all flushed with the newly possible hues and tints: Dubucourt was using aquatint to simulate the aqueous transparencies of watercolour washes. The Gautier D'Agotys with their loudly touted legendary fourth black mezzotint plate were issuing their prurient anatomies, and many another was busily at work at these and other techniques and unheard of combinations of older and newer processes. I worked in various shops and during my stint as one soldier engraver in the army employed on Couché's 'Galerie du Palais Royal'. I was keenly alert for the chance of using my highly developed Teyleresque poupée printing skills and one day unexpectedly the occasion presented itself in the handsome form of Jean Pillement, who wandered into the shop, as artists casually do, seeking fulfilling insights in a work that was near alien to their usages and usually beyond their easy understanding. He had just returned from Poland where he had been painter to the king. Much travelled, sophisticated, widely counted as the finest ornamentist of his day, Pillement was indeed a brilliant inventor of chinoiserie fantasies and

58

floral ornamental programmes of great originality and beauty. We
became instant friends and he disclosed to me his distress at the
crudity and formal misrepresentation in most engraved representations
of his work, and with his generative spurring I began the series of
etched suites printed à la poupée in bright and comely colours after
his beautiful drawings. Our relationship grew from that of painter and
engraver to man and woman and finally to husband and wife. The
wondrous 'Opus Typochromaticum' stayed with me always and it has
long been my hope that it would eventually join the treasures of Sir
Hans Sloane's benefaction to the nation at the Museum Brittanicum.
Pillement grew weary of Paris and longed for his native Lyons, where
we did retire and where I continued etching the cahiers of chinoiseries
and of flowers. I managed a total of forty-five plates, arranged in nine
fascicules, each with a descriptive title page. After Pillement's death in
1808, I returned to England, the 'Opus' bulking large in my baggage. I
picked up the shorn threads of my familial relationships, re-entered
Maria Cosway's circle and am enjoying my declining years, happily at
work and at peace.''

George Stubbs. unpublished etching. 1950.

George Stubbs

At the lonely farmhouse or mill at Horkstow in Lincolnshire, Stubbs labored in the late 1750s, preparing the innumerable drawings that were the foundation of his great book of etchings called *The Anatomy of the Horse* (London, 1776). Working only with Mary Spenser, who is called his common-law wife, Stubbs rigged cables, bars and pulleys to allow him to lift dead horses into the air, to flay them and to draw them, and thus penetrate to the mysteries of equine tissue, muscle and bone. He would need to keep a horse slung into mid-air for as much as six weeks, and the horrendous stench would have driven a lesser artist and a lesser common-law wife from that mill at Horkstow. I daresay that after his laborious years in Lincolnshire a miasmal stench must have hovered over that building, fouling the air for miles about. The drawings are extraordinary, combining power and beauty in their revelation of the intricate and vast structures of the horse. Nothing significant rises up between Ruini's late sixteenth-century Vesalius-like *Anatomia del Cavallo* and Stubbs's *Anatomy of the Horse*, which looms up in alpine grandeur in the huge desert that stretches unendingly between him and the great Venetian Senator. Having completed the stupendous task of finishing the drawings, Stubbs searched for an exemplary engraver to render the drawings into copper and into the possibility of replication. He searched in vain. No one was willing to undertake the arduous, the demanding, the mighty task of transferring Stubbs's magnificent drawings into large copper-plates. In his indomitable way, he did it himself. He set about the gargantuan task of etching the twenty-four plates; they are only slightly smaller than the announced nineteen by fifteen inches. Stubbs, having learned etching to make the embryological plates for Dr Burton, performed with the greatest skill and mastery the achieved prints which are amongst the cherished monuments of graphic art. That self-reliance tells us a great deal about the obdurate, the obstinate, the unyielding George Stubbs, the Stubbs who, with promethean passion and will, strained so powerfully to his purpose that his magnificent *Anatomy of the Horse* is the stupendous issue. Stubbs is of course universally known as the prime painter of horses; he painted many a portrait of racing horses, with the jockey stridently and colorfully mounted, led by the monochromatic trainer. He is the painter of that unforgettable masterwork, "Mares and Foals without a Background", a frieze of horses, the horseflesh all satin and velvet, palpitating with the rhythms, the pulsing subtleties of reality. And beyond the horse, Stubbs was at the dawn of a new and frenzied attitude toward nature, he was one of the (to use Grigson's perfect phrase) "painters of the abyss"; that is, he is a progenitor and early participant in Sturm und Drang: he is in the first rank of English Romanticism. He expressed that Romantic impulse by voyaging into the then-alien precincts of new urban menageries. See those lambent zebras in an imagined landscape, or Dr Hunter's apes, lemurs and monkeys, or the rhinoceros, or Mr Mellon's great gathering of wild imaginings, of horses great and small, being attacked and mauled by ferocious lions. And the wonderful, strange immediacy of "Cheetah and Stag with Two Indians": Stubbs, as Taylor tells us, had no interest in the bizarrie of the Duke of Cumberland's experiment, the stag would have long been away, fleeing for its life; but how vibrantly and freshly the scene comes to life before our thankful eyes. In our image-sated time, when we all have seen films of actual lions, tracking, snaring, killing and devouring prey, our glutted brains and eyes cannot respond to Stubbs's extravagant imaginings as his contemporaries did. If you will forgive that observation, which feels very much like a non-sequitur, I would aver that even we are impressed by the energy, the ferocity, the power of imagination, that flows from these works. Quite different are these disquieting paintings done on the bisque tablets that Stubbs's friend Josiah Wedgwood prepared for him. I am especially attracted to the Tate's "The Haymakers". A group of farm laborers, as though perceived in a dream sequence, are magically stopped in mid-action as they load a great hay wain (an old emblem of the world). I am not suggesting allegorical meanings for this work, Stubbs was doubtlessly interested in hay as the provender of horses; I dare say that nothing equine was alien to him. But the trance-like quality, whether a function of the bisque or an expression of Stubbs's attitude toward farming, is attractively odd. At a very advanced age, at seventy-one years, in fact, Stubbs undertook a work of great difficulty and complexity. He started a dense and intricate work of comparative anatomy, called "A

Stubbs. we. 1960.

Comparative Anatomical Exposition of the Human Body with that of a Tiger and a Common Fowl". One hundred and forty-seven drawings and fifteen stipple engravings survive the exigencies of this happily immoderate undertaking. The death of Stubbs interrupted its completion, but what a noble fragment is ours. Stubbs found a dead panther or leopard at Pidcock's Menagerie, and in the surviving red chalk drawings one can sense his fervid pleasure, his joy in the work of dissecting, of delineating the puissant forms, the juggernaut of power that was now stilled. The drawings and etchings of the human figure seem a bit pallid and unimaginative, uninfused with that Stubbsian drive, that Stubbsian dynamism, that Stubbsian clamor. The chicken is another matter: Stubbs is the quintessential animal painter; he responds to animal forms with a direct freshness, a throbbing intensity, an innovative brilliance. This plucked common fowl invariably makes me think of Diogenes sending off a plucked chicken to Plato, saying, here is the actuality of your observation, "a human being is nothing but a plucked chicken". Those chickens pass from fatted nakedness to skeletal deprivation in a series of brilliant drawings, always consistently masterful and always believable. I was astonishingly fortunate to be privy to the rediscovery of a hoard of these drawings at the Worcester, Massachusetts, Public Library in the early 1950s. The drawings had been deposited at the library by its original benefactor, Dr John Green. Then librarian Thurston Taylor and I were friends, and he phoned to tell of what turned up in a near-complete inventory of the library's holdings, the first since the Thirties. Imagine the excitement, the deeper marveling when the great Stubbs expert Basil Taylor arrived in Worcester, verified and identified the drawings, explained their importance, and indicated their probable intended use. Stubbs, alas and not unexpectedly, died before the completion of the great work. That his purpose was resolute is manifest; further evidence of his massive obduracy can be seen clearly in his portraits by Ozias Humphry; the formidable, obstinate, inflexible, stubborn, iron-willed artist was perennially trenchant from youth to great old age, undertaking the most ferociously difficult tasks, fulfilling his set goals with steady brilliance except when death intervened with its desolate finality.

Salvator Rosa and John Hamilton Mortimer

A cruel wag viciously suggested that the English regarded painting as a branch of literature, which is malicious nonsense. The English love Turner and Whistler, painters of the purest and of an entirely aliterate atmosphere. But the English are also addicted to narrative pictures, they love scenes of unfolding reality, brought to great heights in Hogarth's sequences of novelistic pictures and pertinaciously so, in the truest of pre-Raphaelite painting and in the best of the Victorians, supreme in Orchardson, Grimshaw and Augustus Egg. I shall not go on peddling nor considering a notion so fundamentally specious and so manifestly meritricious; do painters exist of a tendency more literary than Tissot, Meissonier, Gerôme and Bougereau of France or Mackart or Spitzweg of Germany and a host of others from every country? No, the English taste in painting was and is, as elevated and as debased as any other nation's, witness on the elevated side, its great and extensive pictorial holdings, public and private. The English adored Salvator Rosa; their spirit responded to the wilder reaches of Romanticism which tenebrously pulsate from his canvases and to that turbulence in landscape which was especially dear to them, and their sensibilities quickened with delight to the storm-drenched cliffs in Rosa, and to his rock-strewn vistas and voracious and coruscant skies; they decidedly resonated with the banditti-infested landscapes; indeed Mortimer painted Rosa, depicting him as bandit-beggar-philosopher in the accepted, Ribera-tainted tradition of the representations of Democritus and Heraclitus. As early as 1824 Lady Morgan had written *Life and Times of Salvator Rosa*, which further swelled the crescendo of interest evidenced in his work. She noted anent his presumed time with the banditti, "The event which most singularly marked the fearless enterprises of Salvator in the Abruzzi, was his captivity by the banditti, who alone inhabited them, and his temporary (and it is said voluntary) association with those fearful men. That he did live for some time among the picturesque outlaws, whose portraits he has multiplied without end, there is no doubt." Horace Walpole writes about an alpine journey of 1739, "Precipices, torments, wolves, rumblings – Salvator Rosa." Like a vapor, Rosa had invaded the English consciousness. A remarkable letter from Rosa, written on 13

Rosa. etching. 1964.

65

May 1882, notes, "The journey was beyond all description, curious and picturesque: much more so than in the route from here to Florence. There is a strange mixture of savage wildness and domestic scenery, of plain and precipice, such as the eye delights to wander over . . . . O God! how often have I sighed to possess . . . those solitary hermitages which I passed on my way! How often I wished that fortune had reserved for me such a destiny! I saw at Terni (four miles off the highroad) the famous waterfall of the Velino on the river Rieti; an object to satisfy the boldest imagination by its wild beauty, a river dashing down a mountainous precipice of nearly a mile in height, and then flinging up its foam to nearly an equal altitude." One can hardly conceive of Mortimer without the precedent and overlooking Rosa. The manner of Rosa inspired the British for much of the eighteenth century. There was resistance to Rosa, there were those who found their way to Clovian evanescense, to Claude's charged vision of antique purity, bathed in the golden light of a near invisible perfection. Constable, who didn't like him, said of Rosa, "A great favourite with the novel writers, particularly the ladies." Ruskin said he was sickened by "the dragon breath" of evil that infested his paintings and called Rosa a "ruffian and a charlatan". Ruskin who was a deep and sensitive critic, the restorer of Turner, despite the pudendal destruction in the basement of the British Museum, is obviously responding to gossip concerning Rosa's character (the images of that banditti-tainted, lute-playing improvisating poet-painter must have terrified the shrinking, timid, involuted Ruskin). In a celebrated self-portrait, Rosa painted himself trapped in darkest melancholia. He looms in half-figured prominence, dark, dour, his thinnish lips turned down, with the suggestion of a sneer, his deep dark eyes looking all aslant and sidewise. His mien and demeanor are of a menacing order, he regards us with a hostile look, at once baleful, reproachful and tinged with hauteur. Rosa in this deeply shadowed self-portrait leans his right hand against a tablet on which is inscribed in Latin capitals, "AUT TACE AUT LOQUERE MALIORA SILENTIO" which in English warns, "Keep silent unless your speech is better than silence." There were of course many romanticisms and the Rosaesque brand flared and sputtered deep into the nineteenth century. Rosa was amazingly gifted, obviously a very great painter, but contemporary accounts tell us that he was also a superb composer, a fluent performer on both lute and flute, a meritorious poet, and within the tradition of Commedia dell'Arte, a brilliant improvisator of satire. That satirical brilliance caused Rosa a distinct quotient of embitterment. He directed many an improvisational sally at several lesser painters, who in retaliation, managed to "blackball" him from membership in the Roman Academy of St Luke. John Hamilton Mortimer was unhinged by Rosa, who was his sole paradigm, his ever-present model, his stellar praxis. He studied when young at the Duke of Richmond's gallery of antique figures; Mortimer called this his "dead school", the shore of Sussex his "live one". Regarding Mortimer's "living academy", Cunningham in his *The Lives of the Most Eminent British Painters, Sculptors and Architects*, observes, "Bred on the sea-coast, and amid a daring and rugged race of hereditary smugglers, it had pleased his young imagination to walk on the shore when the sea was agitated by storms – to seek out the most sequestered places among the woods and rocks . . . to witness the intrepidity of the contraband adventurers, who, in spite of storms and armed excisemen, pursued their precarious trade, at all hazards . . . from boyhood become familiar with what amateurs of art call, 'Salvator Rosa looking scenes'; he loved to depict the sea chafed and foaming." Cunningham speaks of this rough-shaped, wildly habited coast as "with pirates on water and bandits on land", a lively Rosaesque academy which delivered a profound and unforgettable stamp onto Mortimer and forever after lent his works "a certain dash of savage grandeur". Sometime soon after these native studies, "he was admitted a member of the private academy in St Martin's Lane". Edwards in his *Anecdotes of Painters* further notes, "In these seminaries he acquired very considerable knowledge of the human figure, which he drew in a style superior to most of his contemporaries." "If his drawing owes much to Salvator Rosa, at least it was like taking from like, one violent character pulled to another. And Rosa and Guercino, one should remember, were still almost 'modern' . . ." (G. Grigson, *Painters of the Abyss*). Mortimer's life and works are tangled in uncertainties, in puzzling diversities and in anomalous ambiguities. What is certain is the distinct artistic personality that arises from his paintings and drawings. Everyone attests to the power of his drawings, he painted boldly, (he was wont

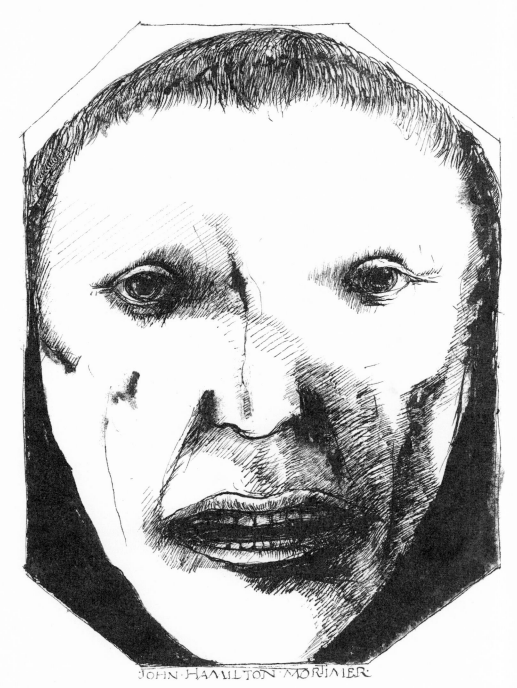

JOHN·HAMILTON·MORTIMER·

Mortimer. drawing. 1987.

to be intense, robust, direct and puissant) both in composition and in coloring. As his painterly oeuvre is revealed, as his lost works are rediscovered and set before our feasting and astonished eyes, his great and original stature will be perceived. He worked much for the publishers and many a volume of plays bears a print engraved after Mortimer. So intense and discriminating a collector as Sir John Soane decorated a room in his Lincoln Inn Fields treasure house with painted roundels by Mortimer of characters from Shakespeare. Frederick Cummings says of Mortimer, "Greatly admired during his life and after his death, Mortimer was described as a latter-day Salvator Rosa, whose works he imitated. He also took subjects from the art of the past, portraying Rosa as a warrior seated in a landscape and studying a book of his own etchings." Fuseli did not like Mortimer as Grigson notes in his brilliant article quoted earlier: "He saw in him too much of Salvator Rosa, and too much no doubt of the Baroque in the vigorous wriggling of his line. In his monsters and in much else Fuseli would have found only the capricious." Fuseli's dislike of Rosa and Mortimer is surprising. He was very like them both in the unremitting love of fustian. Why did Mortimer's monsters displease him? They were of a species akin to his own monstrous creations; perhaps that's why: or perhaps, simple Fuselian dyspepsia. Cunningham observes, "that Fuseli liked none of the English school, spoke with contempt of Hogarth, Gainsborough and Romney – and was much disposed to consider everyone a personal enemy who presumed to paint either poetry or history, which he presumptuously claimed as a province wherein he was sole monarch. He, whose taste was so sublime that he accounted Milton and Shakespeare the only poets of our island, . . ." John Hamilton Mortimer always put one in mind of John Wilmot, the Earl of Rochester, the debauched, brilliant, lewd, salty and lascivious Restoration poet. Like Rochester, Mortimer died young, at the age of thirty-eight; Rochester at thirty-three; both were esteemed as handsome, physically powerful and extravagantly dissolute; both were described as fascinating but dangerous companions, drawn irresistibly to the gnashing centers of tumults and alarums and besotted and wanton and succumbful to all temptations, (deeply inebriated, Rochester in early-morning homeward plod, spotted the new crystal sun-dial which Louis XIV had presented to Charles I. Formed of an obelisk-like base, surmounted by a globe, Rochester shattered it as he pierced it with his sword, shouting, "What! wouldst thou fuck time." For which he was exiled from the court, which missed him and which found him soon reunited with his monarch;) both were excessive in their artistry, which was driven by demon-harnessed energies and both looked deeply into the darkest and most fearsome depths of the Grigsonian abyss.

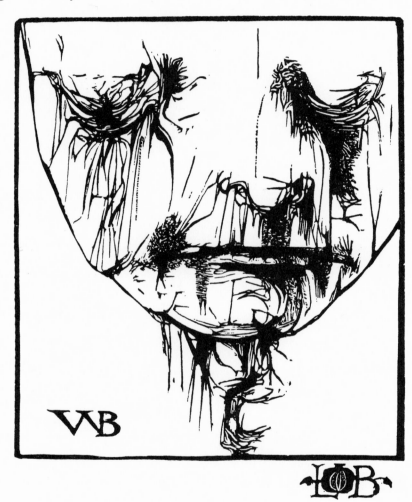

Blake. we. 1956.

William Blake

Blake struck me like a run-away locomotive. The impact was staggering, irresistible and overwhelming. The doubled force of poem and image was numbing in its power and soul-releasing for the glory of its cantillation. I discovered Blake at a crucial junction in my life. I was very young, and irredeemably unhappy in New Haven, suffering the brutish academics of Beaux Arts insensitivity, intransigence and inflexibility, then holding sway at the Yale School of Art. I wanted to draw lightly in pencil, in a hair-raising style that combined Botticelli and Rossetti; and to have my fevered and fervent gentilities overlain with heavy-handed charcoal corrections was more than my exposed sensibilities could bear: my response was to remove myself from the retardiaire fumes of that academy, away, away from the coarse charcoal-wielders to the delicious silence and privacy of the Linonian and Brothers Library, beneficently housed within Sterling. I read voraciously and omnivorously out of a primary need, and in that nutritious context, I first saw Blake plain. My infantile response was mimetic. It was my lucky fortune that the mastery of graphic processes was still in my future, ergo, I did not try to imitate his atypographic manner which has proved essentially inimitable. Instead, under Blake's spell and under his insistent aegis, I taught myself the happy rudiments of that arcane artisanry, printing. "Whence did the wondrous mystic art arise, of writing speech and speaking to the eyes." Three Yale colleges had printing offices and I was allowed to make free with the C & P foot-treadle press at Jonathan Edwards. The office was in a disused gardener's shed in the College's small quadrangle: I printed early and late and made a quick repute as the mad printer of J E. Thus began a life-long communion with Blake, the collecting of all of his works excepting the prophetic books, which are the superb play-books of millionaires. I penetrated as deeply into the Blakean cosmology as I could go without engaging the deepest mysteries of "Fearful Symmetry". I have come to the following eccentric proposition in re Blake's work, which is, that he cannot hold the poetry and the images in a parity of either power or magnificence: the one or the other is inevitably diminished. For example, the wondrous "Tyger", a profoundly original and enduring poem, a poem

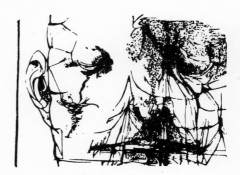

Blake: a fragment, we. 1956.

Blake. unimagined death mask. we. 1956.

whose imperatives engender indomitable power, is accompanied by a clumsy, naive, and forgettable image of a pussy-cat; no equality of means and meaning, no puissant symmetries, no immortal eyes, just that absurd tabby. But when his art is convincing, when it soars with consummate skill and grace, the verse grows dense and throttled by private meanings. Witness the mind-jamming electrical brightness of Urizen, the unfettered clarity of Jerusalem, and what a knot of self-cloning words to unravel, to fathom, to comprehend. The "Explicators" cling to the texts and expose the hidden constructs, explicate them, the infolding interdependencies and deeply cached meanings. But the relief etchings function with eye-enveloping brilliance, they are readily comprehensible, one instantly pierces to the heart of their meanings and intents. "Mad Blake" doubtlessly extended his eccentricities, naturally endowed and with considerable capacity for oddness, stretched to its extreme the borders and beyond of conventional behavior, so that the staid Horace Walpole said of him "Shockingly mad, madder than ever, quite mad." Blake was richly fitted-out with a stock of artistic fakery, fakery for want of the apt word; he feigned near divinity or at least, close acquaintance with the deities, as in this delicious story. Blake was showing a group of his drawings to his supportive friend, the artist Fuseli, a short, fiery man, who was in his paintings and drawings the master of the Burkean horrific. "They are wonderful aren't they?" Blake said. "How do you know that?" Fuseli asked. "The Virgin Mary appeared to me in a vision, and told me so." "Well," said Fuseli, "she does not have immaculate taste." Blake endlessly refined the difficult medium of relief etching, a neo-Primitive means of a very advanced sort; the notion of printing images and words together hearkens back to the blackbooks of the earlier fifteenth century, in which the letters which form the words and the pictures are cut on the same block: Gutenberg, of course, invented movable types. Blake claimed that this rare technique was revealed to him in a dream by his dead brother, Robert; he illustrates this heavenly intervention in the prophetic book, *Milton*, when in the hard, wretched and naked reality, the secret was passed to him by his small patron, George Cumberland. "Fetch me my things," Blake suddenly shouts, "I see the ghost of a flea." For John and Cornelius Varley, and perhaps for a few mugfuls of porter, Blake

72

happily drew a small assemblage of envisioned heads, in range from "The Builder of the Pyramids" to "Edward the Confessor". Blake the seer, the prophet, is humanized by these pranks, his achievement rendered less awesome by these very human idiosyncrasies; a small bridge to his towering and isolated genius is built by these "merrie conceits"; on occasion when calling on Blake, one was told by Catherine Blake, "Sorry, he is not in, he is so often in Paradise, these days." Like late medieval Adamites, William and Catherine were often reported as wandering about their house, entirely naked. Blake was locked into the prevalent neo-Classical modes and mannerisms, those dreadful Flaxmanian flaccidities, that embrace of linear rigidity, which enmeshes forms within a net of steel that has been ruinous to those weaker artists who could not overcome the strangling power of the convention. For Blake, the trap was safely avoided; out of the linear modalities, he fashioned a Michaelangelesque vessel into which he poured the tumult of his artistic and poetic aspirations, desires and visions; that vessel was like an iron-bound sleeve, immutable and unchangeable, but subject to manipulation and exploitation by Blake's genius. He fills the sleeve with the wild power of his imagination, and in his greatest works, the mighty, epochal inventiveness of Urizen and Jerusalem, the device of the sleeve is overlooked. When works of art conform to specific styles and conventions of an era, it is instructive to see how quickly we distinguish the masterly from the ordinary; we do not confuse Salieri with Mozart, Clementi with Beethoven, regardless of similarity of devices and means. Within the boundaries of a given stylistic modality the titan can extend the range of possibility, can plumb the deepest depths of meaning and feeling. Blake is a prime instance of an artist breaking through the artistic constraints of the time. Think of the furore Blake unleashes into those dim outlines, what a Herculean struggle Blake stages within those limp Georgian frameworks. How Blake enlarges the "Night Thoughts" of Edward Young; those endless lines, bowed down in weariness by their turgidity, are ennobled and enriched by Blake's powerful engraved surrounds, animated and monumental by turn, and glorious as instanced in the opening to Book Three, wherein a giant serpent winds itself around the letters and framing linear box, and splendidly disposes itself extravagantly across the entire page. That huge and

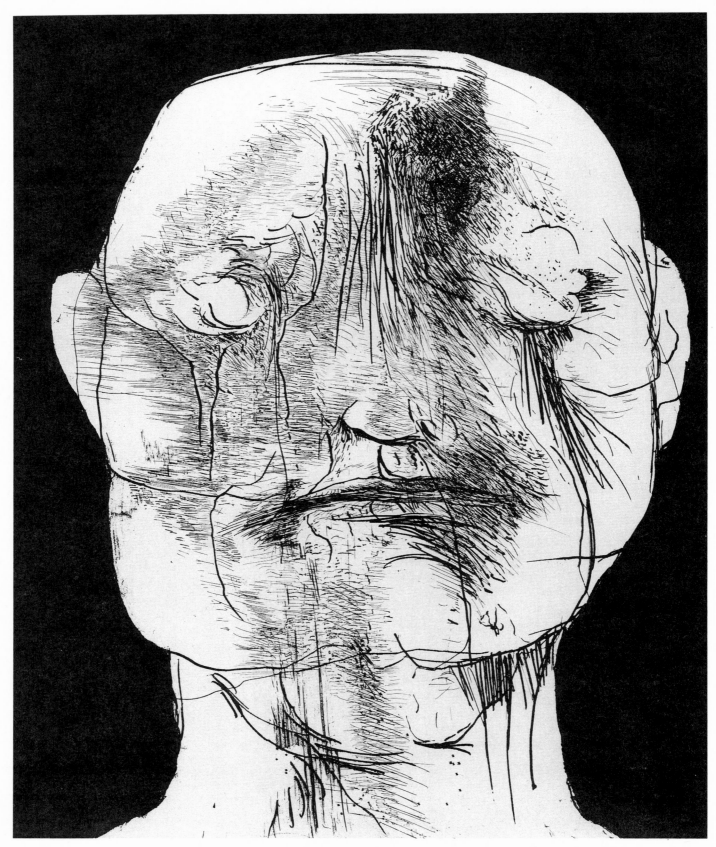

Blake. etching. 1962.

distended snake, rich and vibrant in coloration, is unforgettable and, in its prosaic poetic context, unbelievable; this hot, mammoth incendiary python is mesmerizing and unexpected in Young's cool niceties. Throughout the long work Blake's designs lift the pages to enchantment. There is in Blake's prophetic books a relighting of those long-dampened fires that lit up the pages of medieval books; outline designs are prime objects for coloring, and Blake with Catherine's untiring help painted the colors all ablaze in lineaments of reality and fancy. We are the lucky beneficiaries of those few prescient persons who not only ordered copies of those books and rejected them plain; they would have them colored. Of course, *Milton*, *The Four Zoas*, *America*, *Europe* are masterworks, but even in the earlier *Marriage of Heaven and Hell*, a book whose brilliant originality is perennially and strikingly fresh and is a marvel for the richness of the illumination, even to the filling-out of Blake's lines with tiny rampant horses and human figures variously running, tumbling or reposing. Within the text *A Memorable Fancy* describes a Printing Office in Hell: a description that is primal for me who called his private press Gehenna; the quintessential picturing-forth of the hellish environs of the devil's art, a flash of iconographic inevitability that haunts my memory and remains my ur-image of a printing office. I had the instinctive good sense not to trespass into the sacred province of texts that had received any Blakean illustration or illumination, but to safely raid the unadorned richness of the Pickering and Rossetti manuscripts. For the Print Club of Philadelphia I printed and illustrated Blake's *Auguries of Innocence*, that astonishing aggregation of couplets that strike with poetic frenzy at injustice of all kinds and regard truths with striking novelty: "Naught could so deform the human race/ Like to the armourers iron brace." I have always been intent on making a book of Blake's aphorisms, apothegms and epigrams, and doubtless will, one day. I shall not recite the great works of the divine man but will only haplessly speculate upon the profound and tenacious hold that his works have in our consciousness. They hold sway in the deepest caverns and chasms of our being, where we experience the heights and depths of human misery and exultation. Our perceptions of "Job" are forever conditioned by Blake's set of engravings; it is with inevitable aptness that he captures entirely and perfectly the history of

Blake. from Life mask by Deville. we. 1956.

Job and of his troubles. See the note accompanying the wood-engraved portraits of Palmer for the generative influence enacted by Blake's wood-engravings for an edition of the *Pastorals* of Virgil. The first typographical printing of *The Tyger* occurs in a book of reminiscences about a wunderkind whose remarkable drawings were brought to Blake's notice and presumed admiration. Blake engraved the memorializing portrait of the prodigy, after Romney, I think, with an encadrement entirely of his own devising. The boy's father describes the odd and singular genius Blake; he is not very certain of the creature he has netted and proffers examples of his work and, inter alia, *The Tyger*. In such odd circumstances and under these strange auspices does this masterpiece of English poetry make its first type-printed appearance. In 1956 the Gehenna Press issued *Blake and the Youthful Ancients* in homage to Blake and the young artists who spiritually and actually eased his last years. They accorded him honor, they heaped him with kudos, they looked upon him with awe and wonder, they fed him the honeyed sustenance so crucial to an artist in old age. They, Samuel Palmer, George Richmond, John and Cornelius Varley, Frederick Tathem, Edward Calvert, Francis Fitch and Henry Walters, lauded him as prophet and seer, as the incarnation of his own *Ancient of Days*. They found succor, provender and praxis in Blake and his works; he enabled them a release of poetic sensibility and painterly sentiment that ran counter to the fetters that academic compellant work-to-rules were ever-ready to clamp them into. When the Blakean rays of golden zeal, of driving fervor, of passionate ardor, moved away from them, they relapsed into commonplace dullness. When the Blakean afflatus was directly and powerfully inspiriting them and their works, especially Palmer and Calvert attained a visionary intensity. Blake's penumbral magic mantles and nourishes artists today; they see a universe of possibility in the grandeur and terror of his titanic achievement.

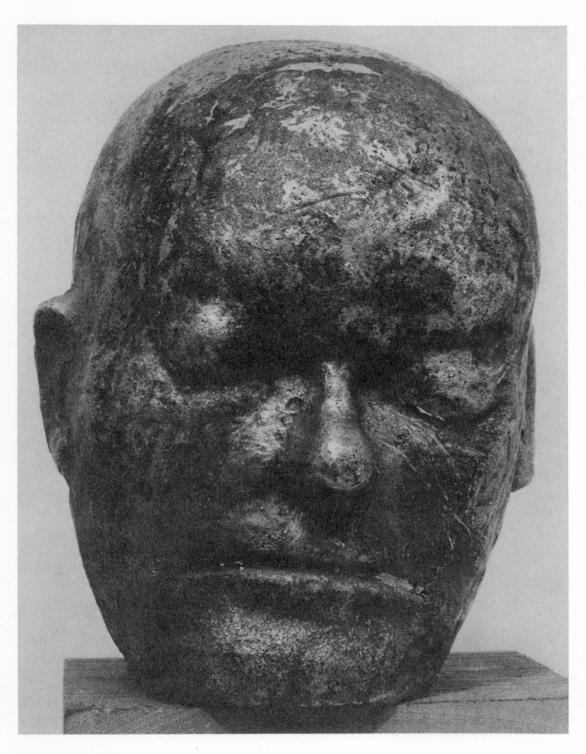

Blake. bronze. 1955.

Palmer. we. 1956.

Palmer. we. 1956.

Samuel Palmer, Edward Calvert and George Richmond

When the English are touched with the divine afflatus they burn with incandescent, white heat. Their geniuses are driven to incredible intensities and wondrous inventiveness; the imagined lifts to the visionary; they are transformed, they produce works of fairest glory. The afflatus can deflate abruptly, the sun stroking Dadd into patricide and the mightiest leaps of fancy; Smart driven by publisher's hectoring niggardliness, poverty and anxiety into jubilation for the Lamb and all-else on earth; Blake, "He is so often in Paradise, these days," said Mrs Blake; and others. That particular "ecstasis" is their specialty: thus Samuel Palmer for three light-bending years, Edward Calvert for a sublime extended small arc of time, and George Richmond for an enchanted moment. For three extravagant years Samuel Palmer painted and drew a landscape lit up to lambency by great, looming, hornéd moons; moons that had not been seen before, these moons rise up and lay their swollen orbs abreast the land, these moons are orange sickles slicing into the depths of star-ridden skies, these gigantic full-moons and their phases are concurrently seen within the golden globes, and the light encrusting the night-embraced sheaves of wheat and blooming trees, makes them shine with an internal brightness. These landscapes and the objects bestrewing them, the lichen-stricken barn roofs, the coruscating stone walls, the trees assuming bizarre night-time shapes and the wondrous day-lit trees, fruited, overladen with flowers, burdened with fruit. These paintings are infused with a range of greens that impinge on a phantasy-dipped landscape. Palmer's six-year exploration of Shoreham as sifted through his exacerbated sensibilities resulted in a series of works unique in English art; they are startling in their eschewal of convention and formulae. When those Shoreham years were up, the moon and the stars were snuffed out, extinguished by a deadly substitution of the ordinary for the hallucinated. Palmer married the daughter of John Linnell, the competent but uninspired landscape painter, the friend and patron of Blake; Linnell somehow managed to clasp his frozen hands into the heart and mind of his son-in-law and helped him be cleansed of, indeed be rid of, that divine afflatus. Off Palmer went to Italy and into a lifetime of banality, except that in the last years of his life he made a series of etchings to illustrate a limited edition of *The Eclogues of Virgil*. Those evanescent moonbeams struck him for a last glowing. Blake had engraved a set of wood-engravings for Thornton's edition of Phillip's translation of the *Pastorals* of Virgil, from which depends a vision of pastoral peace, joyful innocence and amplitude. These small wood-engravings are set into this pedestrian book like a great gemstone in a mass of offal; the book was besotted with a plenitude of indifferent illustrations and the translation of Virgil is wretched. These Blakean wood-engravings had a profound influence on Palmer, and especially on his friends Edward Calvert and George Richmond. The designs Palmer etched at the end of his life return to those fructifying wood-engravings of Blake's; designed in densely layered iterations, stroke after foraging stroke, line after seeking line. Palmer achingly recreates that pastoral vision; the innumerable lines blending into a consistency of blackness, in which a bellman is barely perceivable, a shepherd opens the fold, a tower looms high in a star-filled sky. It is said that his son A. H. Palmer helped in pulling proofs; this idiot son destroyed nineteen of Palmer's twenty sketchbooks. If the others had only a scintilla of the quality of the escaped sketchbook then that son's apish behavior achieves a desecrative level that beggars linguistic equivalents: one can only presume that the destroyed sketchbooks were the equal of that precious survivor. Apparently A. H. Palmer in a paroxysm of Victorian religiosity considered his father's youthful expression of agnosticism too dreadful to survive. Edward Calvert engraved but two handfuls of wood and stone engravings and one copper, directly influenced by Blake's Virgil designs. These small works of Calvert are compressed, intense, wild, exuberant, haunted: they issue from an ardent imagination fixed on those tiny monumental engravings by Blake. But Calvert carries the theme to its ultimate and draws it, pushes it to the perimeter of possibility; in the "Early Ploughman" and "The Cyder Feast" Calvert's vision is of a primal purity, a landscape very dense but unsullied, its people near orgiastic in celebrating harvests, the Dionysian raising of sheep, and the ploughing of the earth. Calvert was trapped in dementia. Unhinged by crazed notions of Greece, which he visited, he painted boring pictures of shepherds and sheep and goats trudging through the Greek ambience; he erected a small altar in the back garden of his London

Richmond. we. 1956.

Palmer. we. 1956.

Calvert. we. 1956.

79

house and sacrificed lambs to Pan. George Richmond painted a small portrait of Palmer, a very intense portrait, making him in the image of Christ, but he enters into these ranks because of three small engravings. He was a friend of Palmer and of Calvert, and the three often roamed about Shoreham at night, drunk on the radiating moon and entangled in the stars: the locals called them the "Astrologers". They all, Palmer, Calvert and Richmond and Walters, Finch and Tathem, paid homage to Blake and lit his last years.

Calvert. we. 1956.

Calvert. we. (enlarged detail). 1956.

Alfred Gilbert

The styles of high Gothic and Art Nouveau would seem to be
fearsomely antithetical, but the disparities are yoked to compatability
in the works of the extraordinary English sculptor Alfred Gilbert. This
fruitful if bizarre compaction is most powerfully and most
magnificently manifested in Gilbert's greatest work, the Duke of
Clarence memorial, crammed into St George's chapel at Windsor
Castle. There is the oddest admixture in Gilbert of artisan, sculptor,
goldsmith, with an overlay of wizardry in his manipulation and
deployment of metals and precious materials. He introduced into
England sophisticated techniques of lost-wax bronze casting. He was
interested in metal alloys, used aluminum in a public sculpture, for
the first time, in the famed statue of "Eros"; he devised new patinas
and patination procedures. Gilbert was obsessed with process and was
in the truest sense a virtuoso of diverse sculptural materials, in consort
and alone. I believe it was Lord Leighton, the President of the Royal
Academy, who, while showing Rodin a Gilbert bronze, said, "In
England, we consider his bronzes the equal to Cellini." Rodin is meant
to have replied, "Only a hundred worlds greater." Gilbert's career was
scorched by the artist's emergent rôle as producer-entrepreneur. His
maturation occurred long before the emergence of the agent-dealer,
who lifted from the artist's back, for heavy recompense, the artist's
necessity of selling his or her work. There developed in tandem with
that humiliating necessity (humiliating because of the unweighable,
unmeasurable depths of subjectivity, at the heart of all artistic
apprehension and appreciation), a tendency for the artist to become a
commodity; buy the painting and buy the painter, for appearances at
salons, soirées, dinner parties, picnics, boat-rides, country week-ends,
and what not else. It is a phenomenon which is not entirely unknown
today; painters at Cape Cod and other summer resorts vie with one
another to entertain and bemuse and entrap big city lawyers, doctors,
et al., into visiting the artists' studios. The poor artists sweat in
anticipated sales, and the buyers are sharply hopeful of voiding the
fifty percent dealer's share. It is a nasty spectacle to see artists abasing
themselves at mighty banquets, playing at mountebankery at various
entertainments; (I happily render-up my dealer's share, to be spared

that debasement). Gilbert moved swiftly from associate membership to full status as a Royal Academician; he achieved that at quite a young age, hugely admired, swept along by the crucial and influential patronage of Lord Leighton and others, and fell violently into the entangling social traps that yawned to snare him. He moved in the delicious but dangerous circles of Wilde and Whistler, became the friend of both Sir Lawrence Alma-Tadema, that lounging lecher in his overheated tepidarium, and of Burne-Jones, the master of the asexual, the elongated and the sinuous. Commissions poured in, an immense house and studio were built to Gilbert's extravagant specifications and demands at Maida Vale, and a rosy future loomed. But Gilbert suffered from a dreadful incapacity to finish his commissioned work; or an unwillingness to bring the work to a consummate realization. He was intolerably cunctative, patrons were reduced to begging for work, which was finally finished and delivered many years after originally promised. There has been much conjecture as to Gilbert's and other artists' inability to finish work. Freud in his analyzing essay on Leonardo suggests his homosexuality as being a determinant factor. Alfred Gilbert was heterosexual. Gilbert, when accosted by the ever dwindling patience of his clients, avers, in pleading letter after pleading letter, that his tardiness was not the issue of neglect, but due to his zealous regard to bring the work to its ultimate fruition, to fulfill his conception, and significantly beyond that, to allow him to exploit the work's inherent ongoing, growing and changing imperatives, to enlarge and develop emergent capacities not perceived until that moment in the work's resolution, alas, years beyond the promised date. Gilbert did not suffer the dread fate of Balzac's hero, he did not carry on working until he ruined the sculpture, but every work has within it the capacity for enlargement, embellishment, enrichment, and can be made subject to endlessly complicating formulations, especially so in the convoluted complexities of Gilbert's work; he indulged in the endless tampering, the continuous raveling that his style allowed, indeed, enjoined. But all artists must declare "finis", for their sanity, the work's need to exist, and the demands of patronage. Gilbert suffered more than any great artist I know of, from the destructive tendency to allow works to remain incomplete, to work on the sculptures until they yielded their ultimate configurations, their

Gilbert. drawing. 1987.

definitive contours, their essences and the totalities attending their projections into finality. Somewhere, perhaps in a letter, Gilbert compared himself to Pygmalion and his works to so many beloved Galateas, an apt comparison. Gilbert's condition, or should one say, disease, led to disastrous ends; he was declared bankrupt and fled into self-exile at Bruges. He remained in Belgium for well over two and a half decades, enduring all of World War One there. He ultimately returned to England, was restored to the Academy, his orders and decorations reinstated; and, upon the completion of the Clarence Memorial and despite George V's detestation of him, Alfred Gilbert was knighted. Paradigms for Gilbert's conception of the Clarence Memorial are spread over the churches and museums of Europe, but one can point to the early Renaissance "Tomb of St Sebaldus", by Peter Vischer, as being influentially prototypic for Gilbert. The St Sebaldus Tomb is grandiosely complex and is probably the crucial source for Gilbert's use of a multileveled grid formula, over which scene and figures and decorative motifs are of varied size and variously deployed. Gilbert's larger monument grew ever more complex as his inconclusiveness allowed his imaginative genius continuous play, creating forms most wondrous for their flowing involutions, the draperies swirling and cavorting to the needs of pure invention. Gilbert arrays his frieze of saints as standing figures, set above a repeating series of mellifluous flambeau-bearing angels. His St George is caparisoned in an odd, sharply projective suit of armor, the bold shell-shapes flare at intersective points, Gilbert claiming that if an armorer were to make an enlarged version of St George's armor as Gilbert designed it, it would fit an adult male. The strange contained figure, sinuous in its shell-encrusted armorial shell, is made of bronze and ivory. The Virgin is robed in silver with touches of gold and other colors. Gilbert describes this sculpture as follows: "I have represented her as standing in the midst of a wild rosebush [purple flowers and golden branches]. . . . Circling her feet, it forms a natural Crown of Thorns, which, sprouting, send their shoots upwards around the figure, in their turn giving off roses to within reach of her clasped hands, where a white lily rises to the touch. Thence the fronds ascend and twine around her head and form a natural crown of full-blown roses." Gilbert skirts alarmingly close to the desperate banalities of kitsch, but his virtuoso manipulative skills and the intensity of his vision save the sculptures. The saintly Elizabeth of Hungary spills her miraculous cloak-full of roses; her architectonic gown reveals the inevitable Gilbertean arabesque, a design derived from Renaissance ornamental systems, modeled in the lowest possible relief, as though fixed onto the bronze with the least means. There are no other sculptures quite like these; they touch tangentially with Fremiet, with Donatello, with Beardsley, with Cellini, with Burne-Jones and with Peter Vischer, a bizarre, a weird conglomeration; but there exists that crucial Gilbertean quotient that subsumes insanely diverse modes into a unique new whole. The Clarence Memorial is further adorned with a statue of St Michael, described by Richard Dorment in these words: "a vespertilionine giant, his great silver-coloured wings spreading down the length of his body, his armour a carapace seemingly composed of feathers and shells. In his left hand St Michael holds a sword almost as big as he is, its hilt forming the scales of the Last Judgement; in his right he cradles a crucifix which he may (or may not) be about to place on the scale, and so save a tiny female sinner from the clutches of a pursuing demon. And the demon itself, like a parody of the angel above, is seen to fly on great bat wings – but, unlike St Michael, to dissolve below the waist into a creature with a fish-tail and terrible claws, wrapping its body around the left-hand balance of the scales." I have never visited St George's Chapel at Windsor Castle and have thus never seen Gilbert's "Clarence Memorial"; but I have steadfastly and constantly if inadequately regarded it in an ever-improving series of photographic reproductions; the most recent being the best and the most detailed, to be found in Richard Dorment's monograph on Gilbert. One is staggered by the complexity of the memorial's conception, the tireless ingenuity of its ornamentation, the power and subtlety of its modeling; its mind-boggling mingling of Victorian insistence on the actual portrait and in full inescapably exact regimentals and wild undulative phantasies, its virtuosic and harmonious mixture of disparate materials, and ultimately the sheer brilliance of lifting the effigy of the memorialized prince, just out of easy sight, to prevent its heavy naturalism to undo Gilbert's complex sculptural and decorative program. Gilbert has written: "I determined to treat the whole work in such a way that its general appearance

should be that of Gothic, yet devoid of the slightest evidence of imitation. This design enabled me to indulge in greater freedom as to the design of the ornamental treatment of those parts where costume had to be dealt with, and also as to the form of the sarcophagus which was to contain the remains of the Duke of Clarence. It will thus be understood why the whole monument takes the form of an altar tomb – a form of shrine, in fact, the sarcophagus being a sacred receptacle, protected by an open-work grille or screen, as is often seen in ancient works, especially Gothic. I decided to treat my offering as a shrine, as a Gothic sculptor would have done, rather than a portrait effigy. In the conception of the pierced work grille, I had in mind the traditional Tree of Jesse – an heraldic allusion to the ancestry and patron saints of the Prince and his house. Thus there came to grow into form representatives of the patron saints of various countries. The recumbent figure was a representation of the dead prince, and had to be a realistic one in order that in future ages his lineaments and clothing should be truthful history. This was a great difficulty. The representation had to be placed at such a height from the symbolic figures that its modern details should not present a jarring note in the whole conception. Another reason for the height of the recumbent figure was the expressed desire of his mother that the remains of the dead prince should rest in mid-air . . . . Many inquiries have been made as to the introduction and also the meaning intended by the treatment of the figure of the Virgin. It is the outcome of reflection upon the nature and character of the Divine Personage . . . . The Virgin is simply draped, with a head covering overshadowing her half-sad expression of features: and she is meant to be in the attitude of resignation rather than that of prayer. The same base that supports St George carries this figure as it does all the others." Mr Joseph Hatton notes, ". . . the lustrous glory of the colours that distinguish their costumes. The shifting light of the sun, or the flickering of memorial candles on them refreshes these with the iridescence of pearls, precious stones and crystals, and what appears to be gorgeous pigment, all toned in accordance with the relative values . . . . I asked him if he would give me some information about the arrangements of colour, in which the art of the painter has been annexed by the sculptor. Mr Gilbert said, 'The colouring of these figures is not paint,

Gilbert. drawing. 1987.

neither is it enamel. It is produced by a medium which by many experiments I thought would serve me well, as it has abundantly proved. As it is composed of oxides and certain liquids, of natural and imperishable lacquers, I have every confidence that it will last forever. Some of the colours are vitreous, though not in the sense that they have been treated by heat. St George occupied two years of steady work. The armour is absolutely an invention. Every detail is so contrived as to be a working model of a suit of armour that could be worn. The shape of its parts and the ornamentation of them are merely a resumé of the entire monument – every line being one which can be found in the smallest detail existing in the rest of the work, which has the appearance of Gothic; and yet I maintain that there is not the slightest resemblance to anything we know of Gothic work, unless the use of shells and other natural forms may be said to have influenced me, as they doubtless did the Gothic craftsmen of mediaeval times.' " Mr Walter Gilbert, no relative to Alfred, recorded the impression he received when he saw the grille surrounding the tomb. Walter Gilbert fashioned the beautiful gates at Buckingham Palace. He wrote, "The grille is really the most wonderful conception, for it is the story of the passage of the soul battling with the wild storms and tempests of life; during the passage the soul is cheered by the promise and signs of hope – the silver figures sparkling in their purity and radiance of the saints, . . . in their lantern-like settings are guiding lights to the mariner on his tempestuous voyage. No artist has ever made so dramatic an appeal to our innermost feelings. When this is realised as it will be in the days to come, Alfred Gilbert will be reckoned as the most poetic sculptor the world has ever had – the greatest because he can play with the fullest throb, those feelings which are divine in us." Alfred Gilbert is the sculptor of the monument which is synonymous with London, namely the "Eros" at Piccadilly, which is a memorial to Lord Shaftsbury. Everyone knows this work, but no one bothers to seriously look at it, to see and perceive it, to note the remarkable Gilbertian qualities of its making. Conceived as a fountain, the soaring figure of Eros is meant to surmount a basin of octagonal design in which water was to play and splash. The "Eros" monument is replete with all of Gilbert's brilliance of design, of the deployment of a relatively simple form coupled to and with a form of elaborate and detailed complexity. The "Eros" became world famous as symbolic of London's surviving the Nazi firebombing, the figure burying its shaft into the London earth, flying through the flames and smoke and overcoming the endless bombing, surviving to reflect the vivid life that floods around it.

Gwen John. drawing. 1986.

Gwen John

There are artists, like Chardin, who abjure the tumultuous, the overweening, the sacerdotal, the searing, the catastrophic, the immense, the scarifying, the anecdotal, the clamorous, the terrific and the horrific: they subsume unto themselves that small patch of muted reality, that preserve of restraint, that outback of quiescence; they paint baskets of strawberries, small jugs of wine, bits of cheese and beer, a corner of a chamber, a chair, a child in the stiffness of shyness, young women displacing as little space as can be, and the sudden sharp perception of an unspoken pain. Gwen John is such a painter, never raising her painterly voice; she has no need to, so sure, so acute, so masterly and so revelatory is her work. Her typical use of color appears limited because the nuances of its manipulation are so dangerously subtle; Gwen John's work sharpens our perceptions, polishes our sensibilities and heightens our understanding. Like the Le Nains, she can force the mundane to glow with obdurant monumentality, and like Chardin she can invest the ordinary, the quotidian, with the charged intensities of grandeur and, like Owen, she sees "heavens in the hollows of wild flowers". Her repressed greys and lilacs caress the shy and the diffident into hesitant sight, her roses and ochres touch with oblique gentleness the adolescent and the child, her murky blues and faded yellows betray the heavy reality of the real world. This mute English swan who wrote Rodin a mass of erotic letters, who posed for his "Eve", turning and bending inwards in a frisson of cold guilt, who had an intense sexual liaison with Rodin, turned to Rilke for both spiritual and human affection. Gwen John was very retiring and very reserved, easily overlooked and set aside, lost in the brilliance flashing from her brother Augustus, who readily acknowledged her greatness. He said in 1946, "Fifty years hence, I shall be remembered only as the brother of Gwen John." Her candor and her honesty, her steadfastness of vision, the eternal clarity of her bounded search and her contained probe, set her onto the road to Parnassus, not at Augustus's expense but rather in despite of his great brilliance. A pearly subdued hue and tone overlays her work and is a participative portion of her work's inimitability. But there is a small group of early works in which a brighter flickering is permitted.

·29·86·   Baskin

John. drawing. 1986.

In the two direct, unflinching, lambent self-portraits of 1900 (Tate) and 1905 (National Portrait Gallery) and in that binary portrait of Fanella Lovell, akin to Goya, nude in one and clothed in the other, the tonalities are considerably less pallid. These and a handful of other paintings form a small sub-division within the corpus of her works. Was it that self-revelation was an entirely secure endeavor? Was it that the mesh of an interior and an exterior, which she knew most minutely and most intimately, unfroze her usual restraint, her more typically oblique approach, her recessive vision all vibrantly aslant, her normal resonance deliciously tangential? In those self-portraits and in her paintings of old friends, Gwen John uses color at once more intense, hues with much greater depth and definition, contrasts that are strong in tint and in tonality. That small cluster of paintings reveal her as almost another painter, freed from the demands of her vast and exhausting restraints. For a short self-declamatory ego-fulfilling moment she calls to us with the clarion colors and forms of pride. It is, however, in the near inexplicability of her works that she lives, as one of the great painters of her age, who thrills us with an almost always muted instrumentality.

Delaune. drawing. 1986.

Etienne Delaune

Does this age suffer from glandular overflow? Does its collective
pituitary suppurate that malaise of giganticism, the artifacts of which
constantly pummel our sensibilities? That rife condition causes artists
to paint enormous canvases, incredible for their vaporous turgidities: a
diseased tumefaction which results in works with content that can be
counted as wanting, in direct proportion to the swelling. Consider
Etienne Delaune, whose entire graphic production – and he engraved
nearly five hundred prints – if mounted contiguously, side to side and
top to bottom, would not cover over a typically bloated painting of the
recent avant-garde. Is this the oversized "whimper" of a dying world?
The last agonized, immense squawk of "anxiety tremens"? Delaune's
tiny works are a blesséd inheritance, and in this age they prick at the
immense tumescences and frame escape vents for the noxious,
gaseous, hot air trapped within them. The printed life of Delaune, as
we know it, would hardly spill over the surfaces of his tiniest
engravings. He was appointed master of the mint at Paris in 1552, and
several beautiful, struck medals of Henri II bear long-established but
unproven attribution to Delaune; and he surely participated in festival
decoration attendant the comings and goings, the marriages and
deaths of kings, queens and princelings. Etienne Delaune is one with
that band of erratic, brilliant, neurotic, elusive, erotic geniuses whose
progenitors fled Florence and made Fontainebleau their heart, and
Francois Premier their prince. Among their principals were Rosso
Fiorentino, Benvenuto Cellini, Francesco Primaticcio, and Francesco
Salviati and in the ranks close behind them, amongst many others,
Hughes Sambin, Rene Boyvin, A. da Trento et alia; Mannerists all: and
among them our delicious little master Etienne Delaune – little only
because the compass of his works was so tiny in size, but of wondrous
complexity. Delaune engraved many series of prints, depicting the
pagan gods of ancient Greece and Rome and the antique heroes,
scenes from the Testaments, sibyls and prophets, martyrs and saints,
intended as models for workers in cameo, silver and gold, enamelers,
jewelry makers and artisans of all kinds; the inventors of such
exemplary works, those books of praxis included such mighty artists
as Dürer and Holbein. The prints are thus gem-like in their small,

Delaune. drawing. 1986.

93

intense, intricate flashing white and blackness. Here is a furious, thrashing Mars, in rich armor, plying his sword against the surrounding crystal, and there is a sinuous, serpentine Diana, bow in hand, treading the ground in her delicate but dangerously demanding way; or in a series of engravings representing the learned arts, Geometry, Architecture, Poesie, etc., we see the symbolic figures all hung about with satyrs and nymphs and grotesques, so beloved of Mannerist artists, and systems of foliage, of scrolls, of strings of pearl-like balls, and of the near-infinite variety of motifs at the command of an expert ornamentalist. In what may be his engraved chef-d'oeuvre, the series depicting "Old Testament Scenes", the murder of Abel, Noah's Ark surmounting the flood-waters, the sacrifice of Isaac, etc., all occur, magically centered under fanciful awnings, recalling the text, "How beautiful are thy tents, O Jacob," at each side a non-illuminating flambeau, brightly but purposelessly burns, assorted animals gambol in the surrounds, where satyrs and nymphs irrationally but delightfully lounge, entirely irrelevant to the vivid, Biblical adventure playing at "stage-center". But I have given no sense of one's delight in the contained extravagance of Delaune's invention, the sure and dulcet ease of the drawing, the happy perfection of the engraving, and all contentedly and securely held within the confines of a human palm, except for a suite of very narrow prints, about one and one-half inches high and about seven or eight inches long, in which armed and armored legions, Roman and otherwise, disport, engaged in the villainies of their wars. Amongst his series of engravings there is a circular set, the prints no larger than one inch in diameter, but one never has any sense of "The Lord's Prayer engraved on the head of a pin"; the virtu is so effortless and the work is so felicitously achieved that one is virtually unaware of the miraculous minuteness of the prints. These perfected works of art participate in several well-ordered traditions, although still within the first hair-raising fifty years of the sixteenth century. A grand iconography of the antique gods was well established, as was a powerful, still developing tradition of ornament, derived from the Roman grottos made more intricate with intervening Moorish and Arabesque motifs; pure ornament prints were etched into iron, in the late fifteenth century, and ornaments printed from woodcuts have an older history. Delaune

94

Delaune. drawing. 1986.

is a master in the first great flush, the first great period of the
fashioning of series of ornamental prints; the tendency continues into
the nineteenth century and beyond. But Delaune's reach extends, on
occasion, beyond the usages of ornament. There is, for instance, a
sequence of small circular engravings celebrating the worship of Henri
II for his earthly moon-goddess Diane de Poitiers. Although we have
no key with which to unlock the prints' emblematic and iconographic
meanings, the human meanings and intentions of deepest love and
the daring compositional invention, along with his other nominated
and celebrated qualities, lift these prints to that level which assures
Delaune a ready acceptance among the greatest Fontainebleau masters.

Courbet. we. 1969.

96

Gustave Courbet

Imagine a Bosch-painted battle-scene; legions of embittered painters
doing arduous battle: all harum-scarum, all darting this way and that,
all hugger-mugger; it is the greasy oil-painters fighting the gesso-
loving, dry-painters in tempera, the maulsticks and brushes at lance
and sword readiness, palettes deployed as shields, bomb-bursts of
paint shells spatter the entire scene in brilliant disorder and disarray:
heading the ranks of the oil-painters like an oleaginous Vercingetorix
is Gustave Courbet, the mighty French master of Realism. Courbet
often paints on a vast scale, a veritable Romantic orchestration of the
pictorial means, witness the immensity of "The Burial at Ornans" or
"The Studio". The leaden strains of a Berlioz threnody seem to allure
the rapt mourners witnessing the burial, all so solemnly tiered in their
dense blackness of garb, the cassocks glowing red in the sluggish
melancholy of the scene. "The Studio" is a considerably more complex
picture in which Courbet ranges his quite definite conception of the
world's good and bad: he places them, the good and the bad in
consort to his left and right; he himself is vested at dead center, being
regarded by the wholesome future in the guise of a young, very fresh,
very pure child, while behind him stands a fleshy nude model,
straightforwardly depicted, not as a seductive odalisque repining in
Turkey finery, but as plain, healthy and virtuous. The picture is full of
surprises: how, for instance, does Beaudelaire, mired as he was in
absinthe and other debauches, get to sit with the good guys? Courbet
painted a host of admirable, compelling and convincing paintings,
making certain scenes and certain formulations his own. Did anyone
paint the sea as purely, directly and consummately before Courbet?
What later was to become a deadly Romantic cliché, Klinger's or
Crane's and doubtless others', animizing the waves into charging
horses, and those swelling, tenebrous, naturalistic representations of
the sea by William Trost Richards and Winslow Homer; these
paintings are suffused with majesty but soon the theme becomes
repetitive, debased and vitiated at the hands of many lesser talents.
And the deep forest glade: here he is extending an existent tradition,
but how he enriches the sudden clearing with deer, hounds and
hunters, alone, in repose, or in action, in the midst of the hunt; how

apt Courbet's fatty oil technique is for these glazed and glowing pictures. How bold and yet how shocking those enormous paintings of enormous young women in bed together, sleeping in suggestive poses or in the act of releasing or dispatching doves; and single female figures, gorgeous and provocative; his eroticism is satisfactory. And a profusion of portraits illuminating his age, Prudhon, Baudelaire, Berlioz, Chopin amongst many others, and boastful, arrogant, cheerful, revelatory self-portraits, that near constant pipe, and in middle age the considerable corpulence of this complex titan. A constant Republican, he was a Communard in 1870, specifically accused of organizing and leading the riot that toppled the column at the Place Vendôme: he was imprisoned in 1871 and went into exile in Switzerland in 1872. How bereft France became to thus lose its great painter Courbet, cut away from his iconographic and cultural heritage, distressed in a foreign environment. He did not long sustain exile; he died in Switzerland six years later.

Bresdin. drawing. 1955.

Rodolphe Bresdin

I have a vision spun out of fancy, of Bresdin instructing Redon,
somewhere in a Carcassonian lay-by, a hidden, dark patch of
Toulouse, the landscape floodlit by the transcendent luminance of
Bresdin. And how electrically alert this astounding pupil is in
attending to his master. In my vaporous imaginings, I see Bresdin
doling out increments from his baggage of pictorial arcana, passing on
his visions of a primeval Arcadia, his North African phantasmagorias,
his abject horror of vacant spaces, the marvels of transmogrification,
the depth of pleasure in the hidden and the lurking and in all of the
over-burdened, as of trees, as of littered rooms and the heavy
emptiness of airlessness, of the encumbered as every surface. Bresdin
didn't paint (Redon's delicacies and subtleties of color has its roots
elsewhere); his artistic requirements were fulfilled by drawing,
etching, and lithographs, of which he made a great number, and
which are extraordinary. Having deeply feasted on Dutch seventeenth-
century etching, Bresdin's graphic odyssey begins in a series of tiny
etchings, all readily distinguished by an uneasy inaccessibility. Small,
overburdened boats and barks sail through heavy, murky, dangerous
seas. Themes that were to reappear in his greatest masterprints occur
from the outset. In his earliest etchings castles, turreted towers and
spires loom unexpectedly, piercing the charged, the seemingly
exhausted air: and hermits occupy their wilderness densities, Holy
families rest in mysterious seclusions, haunted châteaux, as though
spell-bound by Edgar Poe. Bresdin was the prime master of the
minute, no tangle of underbrush was impenetrable to his piercing
etching stylus, no primeval intricacy of forest stayed the flow of his
liquid touch. Bresdin was known as "Le Maitre au Lapin", more, one
presumes, an expression of his manner of living, but there are
accounts of him walking about with a bunny nestled in his arms. He
lived very simply, even rudely, with a pet rabbit in a hut, in a sylvan,
primitive way. Redon describes the vial of Bresdin's magic touche, his
alchemical anxiety anent its purity. Redon tells how concerned Bresdin
was lest a speck of dust distress its purity and distort his intention on
the lithographic stone. Consider his capital work, the lithograph
known as "Le Bon Samaritan". Bresdin was perhaps unique in his

capacity to keep intact the wholeness of a design, despite the near-insane lengths he was capable of in elaborating detail upon unending detail, building it all into a mass of diverting minutiae, into a mountain of whole-destroying bits, and somehow he devises the darkness and the lightness, the near and the far, the large and the small of this design, so that the monstrous tally of eccentric tid-pieces do not wipe one another out: it is an incredible achievement. Is it the prowess of dementia? I think not; no disordered mind could conceivably hold together and build to a meaning larger than its near-infinite parts, the eye-boggling variety, the alpha and omega of the natural world that is here crammed together. It was a quite endlessly diverting game that my children and I played with an impression of "The Good Samaritan". We would peer deeply into the interstitial complexities of this mazelike lithograph, the incredible groups of lemurs that lurk here and there, the thousands of birds that litter the sky, the great depth and height and variety of trees that flourish within the print; rats run along the limbs of sinking trees, dogs drink at sedgeside, startling cranes and ducks, lizards and great crocodiles grow out of the ends of limbs and stumps of overridden and overgrown trees, and in a sudden, an inexplicable clearing the scene of the Samaritan doing his good work, the tableaux dominated by the strange, besaddled, much hung, over-bedecked camel. The ambience is charged and hallucinated, the air is very thin, the atmosphere is exhausted and trancelike, the charged and awesome vapories of reality, a reality that lurked in the vision-haunted mind of Rodolphe Bresdin. How readily and easily one loses oneself into the labyrinthine web of this wondrous print. The mighty festooned trees, thrust ever upward, they embroider the air with infinite numbers of vibrating leaves. And the myriads of birds that flock from tree to awesome tree. And the clouds credibly rolling into friendly but distant skies: and how bewildering to discover behind the tableau-vivant of the Good Samaritan, an army moving over hills and through valleys, and beyond them, miles away, Jerusalem, the city apprehended and explicated in a minute network of lines. Despite the tales of Bresdin's magical lithographic fluid, it is beyond easy belief to think that "Le Bon Samaritan" and other exquisitely detailed prints could have been drawn with the requisite grease on Bavarian limestone. It had been

·RODOLPHE·BRESDIN·

Bresdin. drawing. 1955.

supposed that Bresdin etched his minutiae-overladen visions into copper and transferred the etched image onto the stone where he could further scrape and scratch to an incredible fineness. He could build new forms with his alchemical touch, and he could then refine the newer work with more scraping; it is a procedure entirely sympathetic to so obsessive a phantasist. Several slightly differing versions of "Interior Flamande" exist as etchings and as lithographs; they bear testimony of Bresdin's cross-fertilizing techniques. Bresdin dreamed of the virgin forest, his arcadian visions spurred by deep reading of Fenimore Cooper. He was the subject of a Chamfleurey novel called *Chine-caillou*, which became his nickname, the source being Cooper's Mohican Chingachgook. Bresdin did make a trip to the primeval world. He won a competition for the design of a Canadian banknote and sailed away to Canada to execute it. It is impossible to detect any influence in Bresdin's work of his journey to the new world. Those vast American forests are nowhere in evidence, and his drawings of Indians and Indian artifacts betray more of source books on the Indian than any active confrontation or intimacy or even of any direct experience of the Indian. Indeed it is best to perceive Bresdin as Redon saw him, poetically transformed into "Le Liseur". A lambent old man, emitting his own light, sits in a dark room, a grand book open on the table before him; but this old, this timeless man is deep in reverie; it is Bresdin dreaming the phantasmagoria of enchanted mansions and distant cities caught in mountainous crags, of trembling rests on the flight to Egypt, or Arabs, horsed warriors and hugely costumed women, vast battle scenes of unknown armies clashing anonymously and murderously in a landscape exhumed of air, of chasms, of mountain sides, of forest depths. He sits there, at "Le Fosse aux Lions" indifferent to the tumult of academies and salons refused and otherwise, alone, inimitable, seeing in the enhanced darkness the visions that his hands make palpable.

Rodolphe Bresdin. Machaerium. 1954.

Honoré Daumier

The greatest artists are not readily plumbed nor contained, nor easily categorized, nor reduced to an invariable schema, nor swiftly perceived nor classified. They tend in their grandeur to be multi-furcated, their bevels of diverse mastery flashing to our pleasure. They, like uncontrollable fires, break out again and anew in unexpected areas and with alarming, unexpected strength. It is not a truism of all masters to say that they moved with ease and greatness in all media: indeed, there were those like Giambologna who leave us no corpus of prints and others like Piranesi who left no sculptures: Hollar only etched, Romako only painted, but Honoré Daumier was painter, sculptor, draughtsman and printmaker. Daumier, the divine author of the "Chambre Legislatif", was the penetrating master of human physiognomy, the mighty depicter of our passions, he who held secure the measure of human frailty, of human sympathies, strengths, of human weakness and foibles. This doyen of all that is furtive, hidden, mean, debilitative in human intercourse, this tearer away of veils that protect the usurious, the noxious, the despoiler and the exploiter, Daumier was privy to the usages of deceit, of pomposity, of dissimulation and of selfish indulgence. He pictured with astonishing accuracy the depths of human depravity, one might verily say that all human activity, droll, tragic, comic, satiric, the worlds of art, medicine, the theater, history, were his subject, and he depicted the lives of those who toil in the murky half-lights. Daumier the master of human affect never submitted his face, the constellation of his features, to that discerning, searching probity: he never painted, or lithographed, or drew a self-portrait. It would be difficult to think of an artist of any stature who did not paint or sculpt her or him self, however covertly. Dieric Bouts hides behind a column, a lax servitor perhaps at a last supper. Many an artist peeps out at us from crowded scenes of veneration, some become active players in historical tableaux, a few show us their backs, but very few ignore themselves entirely. But Daumier, the arch portrayer of human emotion, for whom the greatest subtlety of human expression was stock in trade, somehow managed to avoid the depiction of himself. It is altogether very odd that his persona, his hot being, should not have wildly

104

interested him, especially as the world of artists and their patrons was apparently dear to him. He painted artists at their easels, showing their works in their studios; did many paintings and several series of prints of connoisseurs and amateurs; explored the visits of the people to the salons; the ambience of artists' studios was a subject close and dear to him. One is bewildered at the neglect of this wondrous artist to paint himself. Daumier had a powerful tie with Rembrandt; that paradigm's insistent instance was to be reckoned with, and an exemplar to be emulated. It is difficult to understand how Daumier could have avoided painting himself. The truth to tell is that I have been exaggerating. He appears but very well disguised in several prints. There is a self-portrait! A sculpture, in plaster, done in middle years, and that is apparently the only trespass he allowed against his phiz, which was photographed and caricatured by his friends Nadar and Crajat. That self-portrait sculpture is very unlike his other sculptures, which are overwhelming savage caricatures, of the gross denizens of the legislature, the powerful single standing figure of the wretch Ratapoil, and the large relief "Refugees", a theme he explored in paintings and drawings of trenchant and emotion-draining power. The self-portrait sculpture in contrast to these seems classical, is a tight, irrelevant, non-committal, non-revelatory work. That self-portrait sculpture sits about his personality like a skin-tight mask, telling us nothing about Daumier except for the temporal accidence and happenstance of appearance. That self-portrait, in fact, thrusts us away from his inner, the unique being we call Honoré Daumier. Very odd.

Camille Corot

Corot's name is indivisibly united to that near endless series of landscapes that have so tutored nature to have become in themselves a species of actuality, an invention that ventures into the precincts of fabricated reality. These landscapes have entered into the common visual unconscious; we recognize the configuration on sight, whether on canvas or in nature. That usurpation of the natural, that superimposition of a particular vision onto the actual is given to few artists, and yet that is not the crucial agency in our admiration of Corot. It is universally averred that Camille Corot was untowardly generous, magnanimously so by the usual standard; he was especially beneficent to artists, as witness the instance of Paul Desiré Trouillebert, an indifferent follower of the master, whose drawings and paintings Corot is known to have signed to enable the distraught Trouillebert to raise funds. Daumier's beautiful drawing of the aged Corot, benignly dozing in sun-dappled ease, betrays much of the tender affection in which he was held. And nor yet the stupefying atypicality of Corot's behavior attracts him to me; artists are perforce selfish, notoriously so, clinging to their perpetually expanding egos in a time and ambience which they invariably perceive as frozen and alien. It is the figure paintings that compel my interest; they are astonishingly monumental, aloof, suffused, silvery with subdued hues as though hewn from a grey-silver-stoniness, quiet and still, filling with amplitude the restricting edges of the canvas. These paintings are usually of women, who tend to be in repose, sitting, leaning and reclining. They are the heirs to Chardin's monumental quotidianness. Corot's sylvan landscapes, all a compaction of airy wisps, forest glades, trees, wind-blown or still, make play-patterns of sun and shade; the effect is inevitably ephemeral and momentary. But the figures are composed in self-containing positions and settings; they are silent, contemplative, non-gesturing, non-hortatory, self-engrossed, restrained, absorbed: all clanging fractious furore is here banished, and although the air is not enchanted, it is sufficiently strained and straitened and heightened to allow these figures obdurance and endurance, density and weight. Thus they are in some measure kin to the single figures in Vermeer's paintings: devised with different means

Corot. we. 1969.

and sifted through different sensibilities, yet the figures share that timeless beauty of observed truth, made motionless in the keenness of perception, made permanent by the powers of description. As though that did not suffice, there is yet another side to Corot's genius: those crystalline landscapes which he painted in Rome and in French cities convince us that a veil of haze has been pierced and the landscape furnished anew, the view perceived with a reality-enhancing freshness, the clarity of the apperception, the purity of the color and the seeming simplicity of means confer a timeless monumentality similar to his painting of figures.

Carriere. etching [touched]. 1969.

110

Eugène Carrière

Rodin said of Eugène Carrière, "He was the greatest artist of the nineteenth century", a startling encomium from a universally celebrated artist of another, whose repute is essentially wrapped away in the shrouds of specialists. Rodin, playing that delicious, if mindless, game of primacy, places Carrière at that dizzying acme, above Ingres and Delacroix, Géricault and Courbet, above Manet, Fantin-Latour and the host of Impressionists and their close and distant followers, Degas, Gauguin and Lautrec, and the "Beaux Arts" academicians, above Gerôme, Bougereau and Tissot, now being manipulated into the expensive first rank by dealers suffering the want of first-rate saleable goods. And Rodin placed Carrière beyond Carpeaux and Falguiere, Rude and Dalou: an astonishing evaluation. I am content for Carrière not to be the greatest artist of his era, and will consider him in the splendor of his isolation, his style and manner dependent on no one and succeeded by no eminent pupils. Carrière used heated wax as the bonding agent in his oil paintings, an ancient technique known as encaustic; he was also much given to the dread use of bitumen, which has spread a discordant darkness over many a bright picture. Alas, we cannot participate in Carrière's original color conceptions, we see his paintings shipwrecked into the brown distress of bitumen poisoning. But what a glorious wreck. He was the supreme master of "sfumato", that tendency which at its worst tends to smudge, and at its best to fuse all forms into a larger encompassing vision; sfumato decries outlines and borders, it abjures edges, it intertwines forms, it envelopes all shapes into a penetrable smoky veil, to perceive the world as though through a golden haze; these phrases cannot conjure the fundamental poetic mystery that divine fudging entails. Carrière was obsessed with the themes of motherhood, the secularizing mother and child which emerges as a pictorial subject in nineteenth-century art; these are no virginal mothers with infant Christs, but women and children clasped in the deep embrace of burgeoning bourgeois familial love. One would, I think, look in vain in eighteenth-century painting for depictions of profane mothers caressing and adoring and loving their profane infants. There is, I dare suggest, a heightening spirituality, a kind of substitution of religiosity for the affects of love,

111

the adoration of the actual and palpable for the mystic ideal: this finds further expression in the beautiful and unique aquatints of Mary Cassat and, in a strange new way, in the distraught works of Georg Minne, and many another artist. Was this a painterly concomitant to the concerned interest expressed in the works of Pestalozzi and Montessori? Carrière painted an ambiguous self-portrait quizzical, uncertain and emotionally dubious; he surveys the world as though in some pain and distress, the head stiffly lifted and half-turned, away perhaps, from the brutalities of his transforming century. But Carrière's turning-away is not a testament of pictorial superiority, or of painterly hauteur, or even of an attitude of "art pour l'art" indifference; no, he was a person of his times, painting his suffused vision with consistent mastery. He made a series of lithographs, a technique that allowed him the softest of focus, a technique that encourages a greasy irresolution of forms folding into other forms, a technique that allowed the merging of tonalities into a murky, yet penetrable screen. Lithography gave Carrière further allowance to apprehend the world as though through a benevolent layer of vapors, of a vision decidedly penumbral. His lithographic portrait of Verlaine is very famous, which for all the subterfuge of sfumato manages an intense, insistent, direct and sharp portrayal of the quirky, dissolute, great poet, as do his printed portraits of Mirabeau and de Goncourt; they reveal their succinct and eccentric personalities, they shine through Carrière's stylistic proclivities. He is, for convenience sake, set amongst the Symbolists, with whom he has naught in consort, except a decided non-academicism, a reaching for newer means, and an extending vision. Rodin's estimate must be attributed to profound friendship and to the heightened appreciation of familiarity. Carrière is not the greatest artist of the nineteenth century, no one is; he is a painter of originality, of ardor, of great depth, he enlarges our understanding and our insight into his time and he produced painting of deep and lasting beauty.

Theodore Géricault

Theodore Géricault's death mask displays a face eaten-up by
anguished pain. There is barely a trace left of the handsome, vigorous,
dashing young painter who regards us so possessedly in his self-
portraits. Those long, harrowing days in desuetude have registered a
network of misery, pathways revealing the ongoing ransacking of his
flesh. The strong Byronic aspect has been reduced to a system of
marks describing with horrid accuracy the dread decline, the slide into
the grave. The mask reveals a face distorted into mishape; it betrays
the horrid lineaments of debauch or grievous pain. There is a
trenchant entry in Delacroix's *Journal* for December 1823. "Some days
ago I was at Géricault's in the evening. What a sad time! He is dying –
his emaciation is horrible. His thighs are as big as my arms. His head
is that of an aged and dying man. I sincerely want him to live, but I
no longer have hope. What a frightful change." Géricault had studied
in drawings and a painting a decomposing severed human head.
Géricault had acquired the detached head of a thief from the Dicêtre, a
prison, a lunatic asylum and a sometime home for the aged. It is
reported that he kept the head for fifteen days, on the rooftop of his
studio on the Rue des Martyrs, drawing it, observing it, and painting
it. The horrific usually impels nausea, distress, terror, disgust, and
angry indifference. It is inherent and inevitable in Grand Guignol and
in waxworks; it is very rarely seen in the province of the fine arts.
Géricault's numerous paintings of dismembered parts of the human
body are perhaps unique in Western art. They are, of course,
disturbing, hideously so, but so deep is Géricault's passion for the
structure of humanity, so palpable the honest intensity of his desire to
penetrate to the impactive hidden essence, so great his need to pass
through to innermost connective articulations, that the affective
horrific is obviated. These strange, compulsive paintings violently
compel our undivided notice, they demand our attention; they stray
far beyond the bulwark of the expected, the ordinary, the usual. It is I
think Géricault's consummate mastery that lifts the dreadful human
shards out of the gimcrackery of bohemian stews, out and far beyond
atelier knickknackery and studio pranks. The paintings are veritable
"nature-mortes", parts of legs and arms, severed heads in one, feet

113

and hands in another, and various dispositions of catastrophic amputating in a score or more of works. These remarkable paintings are in the tradition of Rembrandt's butchered oxen, of Soutine's dead, plucked and hung chickens, and more recently of Hyman Bloom's "Abbatoirs". There is in all of these pictures of animal slaughter a quality that is disturbingly referential to human beings. Rembrandt bathes his hung carcass of an ox in that glow of golden light, reserved for his most somber human portraits, as though a deep human experience was impending, as though revelation was intending. Was Rembrandt perhaps postulating a beheaded human carcass, in similar circumstance? There is the towering sameness of blood and sinew, guts and tissue, muscle and bone, grease, membrane, tendon. The Rembrandt and the Soutine despite their brutishness do not appall us, they move us; the paintings reach into rarely touched recesses where our understanding of our common humanity is stored. The Géricaults and the others are difficult paintings, unpretty and uncompromising, and they strike at the heart of our vulnerable humanness; they illuminate our sodality of fleshiness, they reveal our unrelenting beefiness to ourselves. Those devastating and wondrous studies of Géricault tear aside the successive veils that hide the universal yet miraculous structures that gird us, that allow us to stand upright, that sustain thought. The ignoble fragments are thus ennobled, the perilous and the putrefying are now allied to a larger cause, to make a new visualization of the whole human being, to render and endow that whole with a persuasive tangibility. Géricault interests me, beyond the vast and the mighty "Raft of the Medusa", that resplendent masterwork so hugely visible at the Louvre, for the series of paintings setting forth the outward semblance of inner chaos, the appearance of aberrant personality, the visible expression of insanity. Since antiquity the representation of character and personality has occupied painters and philosophers. Theophrastus in his *Characteristicos* attempted a complex schema, an ordering into classes and orders of the diversities of personality: a task which just now, one fervently hopes, is being abandoned. Della Porta in the mid-Renaissance concocted a fanciful proposition of the likeness in character and physiognomy of humans and animals, with fantastical engravings pairing humanized animals and animalized humans:

114

Géricault. etching. 1969.

Clemenceau the tiger and Churchill the bulldog are latter-day
expressions of this notion. The French classicizing painter Charles
Lebrun seized upon the whole range of human emotion and tried to
compact that immense variety into an immutable series of images. The
results, endlessly republished, ramified continuously; Lebrun cast a
long shadow; the attempt at categorization was obviously placatory
and palliative and tended toward stereotyping; these reductive
simplications pleased and satisfied successive generations, for well
over two hundred years. However powerful Lebrun's inventiveness,
the results are woefully lacking in depths of revelation, wanting in
insightful subtlety, hopelessly inadequate to the needs of the task,
particularly as perceived from this vantage of knowledge, insight, and
understanding. Lebrun had invented a typological gallery, each figure
expressing a specific emotion as revealed in precisely how the facial
features organized themselves. Thus there were "the miserly one",
"the haughty one", "the choleric one", and many others. These types
are reiterated in immense learned works such as Lavater's multi-
volumed *Physiognomy* and crudely in coarse woodcuts, printed and
reprinted in the chapbooks. The attempt to correlate the structure of a
human face with intelligence, character, and personality was
perpetuated in several photographic works, the most famous being the
intriguing electronic oddities in Duchene de Bologne's treatise. Darwin
and others were very interested in facial arrangement in the
expression of emotions, prefiguring the absurd morphologies of
Lombroso and others. Géricault painted at the behest of Dr Georget
"le medicin alieniste Parisien bien connu", a series of twelve portraits
of bedlamites that form a cabinet of psychological penetration and
insight. Although the commission was cast in the familiar
Lebrunesque mode, Géricault's paintings are subtle, probing,
evocative, and profoundly human in their implications. Géricault's
paintings depart from schematic hysteria and melodrama; no frantic
posturing, no hair-pulling, no histrionic facial displays, and no
depiction of harrowing disorder, or scenes of mayhem or bedlamite
scenographic displays or lunatic asylum bizarries. No, Géricault's
remarkable portrayals seek to convey the mental disarray of his
subjects by exploiting the smallest nuances of physiognomic distortion.
These are subtle and moving depictions of mental illness, no aberrant

116

catatonia, no flamboyant paranoia, no frenzy, just a whiteness about the lips, a bit too much eyeball showing as in the Smith College Museum "Youth". The laugh of "The Old Woman" is entirely inner in its reverberation; these are portraits of people withdrawn into the private corridors of madness, the exclusive insularity of psychosis. Géricault's restraint is wonderful, his deployment of attitude and gesture of the subtlest and the most restrained. These twelve paintings are miracles of subtle understatement; our post-Freudian sensibilities respond and reverberate to the affective nuance that skims off the surfaces and, indeed, permeates these portrayals; we are stunned by the justness of the depictions. What is perhaps most astounding is how far beyond the alienist's perception and understanding Géricault is capable of attaining: that divine afflatus that drove his genius to the achievement of the "Raft of the Medusa", the glorious apex of history-painting, caused all of his works to be infused with profound and generalizing understanding. It is in the nature of genius of Géricault's standard to be protean.

Theodule Ribot

Ribot's "Un Orphelinat" is a strange, haunted and bizarre painting; its children seem like agéd dolls, their fleshy heads almost universally too large, lending an air of frightened unreality to the somber scene. There is a seeming absence of color except for those Ribotesque hushed hues of brown and grey, the tones as though seeped away from fog-drenched dunes; a touch of yellow, a smudge of reddishness; but how the painted tonalities build the little figures into tesserae-like structures. Those orphaned children are locked forever in their indecent, joyless world, an ambience hung with successive layers of dun, of grey, of black. What an extraordinary painter Theodule Ribot is, how he explicates reality with a minimum of signs and symbols, no cries, no alarums, only nods and winks and deft sleights. A cutlet, a jug, a pinched face, an apprentice chef all in white; he is a minimalist in means and a universalist in meaning. How his dark, middle-toned pictures shine and glow, bitumen and all, in a gallery filled with retina-obsessed, mindless Impressionists. Turgid, rosy Renoirs and boring predictable Sisleys betray their bourgeois, their cow-like contentment, but Ribot shines his light into the dimly lit, unrecorded corners of his time. If the great Manet's pictures impelled Courbet to mutter, "Too many Spaniards," I cannot imagine his response to Ribot, whose art is massively concocted out of Velazquez and Ribera. It is from that dark blaze, that enchanted world of shining blackness that Ribot's painting derives, its imperatives directly derivative from Ribera. Ribot was massively interested in the kitchen, and he used its variegated life, its manifold levels and its diverse activities as the subjects of many of his works. He painted still-lives of meats and fruits and vegetables, the brazen and porcelain culinary utensils, but principally he painted a hierarchy of chefs and cooks and sauciers and bakers and patisseurs, reveling in the whiteness of their outfits, contrasting their uniforms and costumes. Ribot's brush pokes into the darkest recesses of the kitchen; he was, if you will indulge me, a Zola of the kitchen; but no ongoing serials and spirals of tales unfold, no naturalistic renderings of generations of cooks; but rather, in their entirety, the many paintings compose realist structures that enlarge on life in and about French nineteenth-century kitchens. It is not the mad

Ribot. wood engraving (touched). 1969.

119

world of Peake's kitchen that Ribot paints, nor are these Piranesian scenes of disorder and disquietude; this is the gross and greasy world of the French bourgeoisie. In the manner of his mentor Ribera, Ribot also made religious paintings; I have never seen any, they are only known to me from contemporary reproductive engravings: knowing his palette and his intensity one presumes that they are deeply felt and inevitably moving. Theodule Ribot painted a marvelous portrait of an old woman; it was the pivotal picture in the paneled library at 19 Gramercy Square, New York City; again the Ribotesque matrix of hues, but out of that manipulation of deepest browns and highest silvery greys glows forth the head and shoulders of the vieillard, convincingly realized, strong and enduring. And one has seen a very Brouwer-like head of a peasant, wearing an odd conical hat and a half-length of a youth, fresh and vibrant. In a house in London are hung many paintings by Ribot and by Bonvin, a contemporary who worked in a related manner; I have visited that house only once, but its glowing walls are resplendent in my memory. Unlike the Impressionists who only painted what their retinas accidentally trapped, Ribot transformed what he saw into a consistent vision of the world, or that portion which interested him, as he perceived and understood it. We are deeply enriched by those subtle, persistent, revealing layers of tonality and line.

Chaim Soutine

Chaim Soutine is wild, passionate, dissolute, explosive, expressive, fervid, intense, expressionistic, irritative, incessant, excited, compassionate, incisive, brutal, incandescent, fevered, demonic, shrill, impactive, coercive, repetitive, compulsive. He is the Bulgarian Jew loosed into the debaucheries of Paris and becoming one of its prime movers. Not unlike the Romanian Jew, Pascin, who plunged insatiably into the perfervid inter-war dissolution – whose brilliance as an artist could not sustain him – he died in Havana, by his own hand. Soutine's dead hanging chickens are icons in dire semblance to ourselves; it is us gasping, eviscerated, plucked, flailing our flightless wings in feeble, desperate protest, the white-yellow fat extruded in sacrificial angst. Soutine's dead, big, flayed beef-cattle enlarge the dimensions of our sanguinity; they define our bodily mansions, those structures of guts and sinew, of tissue and bone which sustain our consciousnesses and our holy souls. The vivid, colored strokes flicker and prance across the canvases, convulsive forms appear and disappear, in speckled array and disarray, with flamelike double dappling. There is in Soutine's red-garbed choristers a garbled memory of the sudden flush of scarlet in the steeped blackness of Courbet's "Burial at Ornans". Soutine is the inevitable heir to Courbet, painting with that oily richness, reveling in Courbet's greasy conventions. Here are no muted, dry, subtleties of Cubism, no pellucid, controlled, intermingling of hues, here is the driving force of unfettered passion, an ecstatic foreclosure on death's blatant scrawniness and the celebratory hosannahs attendant on life's fleshy pertinancy. Soutine was part of the so-called Ecole de Juif, an uncollected group of artists at work in Paris, just before and after the First World War; how unlike Modigliani and Kishing Soutine is, how visibly his fuse sputters, how utterly without protective side or guile he is and, like all true Expressionists, successful and unsuccessful pictures are the happenstance of paint frenetically flung at the canvas. The impetuous furore, the hot, barely controllable, consummation of the object in the act of painting, characteristic of Expressionism, is palpable in Soutine's anguish of foraging in painted jabs and dabs to passionately engulf, to embrace, to consume what is painted. In "an

121

Soutine. etching. 1970.

ecstacy of fumbling" the paint is urged onto the canvas; a tumult of strokes exactly cohere to the violent emotions that relentlessly thrash in the artist's heart and brain. All true Expressionists are in bondage to their exacerbated emotions, all must be quick, instantaneous, seized upon, discharged at once; there is no slow mulling, no considered, gentle changes, no contained deepenings, no Cezannesque mutterings after one hundred and seventeen sittings by Vollard, "The shirtfront begins to please me." No, it must all be a tangled jumble of exposed nerve and of explosive action. It is no wonder that his paroxysm of activity results in works quite out of the intention and control of the Expressionist painter. It is testimony to Soutine's genius that despite the quick, intense, unstoppable applications of the paint, his pictures more frequently than not are successful. How masterful his paintings are.

123

Jan Gossaert, called Mabuse

There is no general agreement that Jan Gossaert was a hair fetishist,
indeed, it seems to have occurred to no one but me; but in his
paintings and drawings hair tends to abound in dangerous luxury. His
provocative Eves are festooned with waves of cascading hair, his
Magdalenes and their penitences are perceived through skeins of thick
abundant hair. These dense glossy garlands of hair are unique to
Mabuse, who might be described as a Gothic Mannerist; the
oxymoronic bizarrie of that notion is made manifest in the work's
rootedness in the splendid stiffnesses of the Flemish fourteenth-
century lurching toward the erotic sinuosities of Mannerism. This
anomalous duality is perhaps best seen in the five drawings of Adam
and Eve from his hand. In these drawings the always hirsute
progenitors of humankind reach excitedly for one another, dangle
together, dispose themselves in amorous abandonment, arch and
touch each other: a quite incredible set of drawings, compacted of
incisive Flemish timidity, Renaissance audacity and Mannerist
neuroticism: drawings washed by the sweet harmonies of Roger van
der Weyden, touched by Dürer's hard, adamantine, and unremittent
gaze and prophetic of Bartolemeus Spranger's turbulent eroticism;
drawings entirely unique for their time and place. Jan Gossaert is one
of those rare bridging and stretching artists, deeply rooted in the past
yet wondrously probing into the future. A portrait of him at the
Currier Gallery in Manchester, New Hampshire, displays a clear-eyed,
large-hatted, intense man, entirely shaved. Odd. Not true, but the
beard is so neatly trimmed and combed to a non-Mabusian neatness,
that I did not remember the beard.

Mabuse. woodcut. 1963.

Pieter Breughel I

When one walks into the immense gallery in the Kunsthistorisches Museum at Vienna, where half the world's extant Breughels are hung, one's heart leaps at the recognized scenes, the recovered images. It is a swoon-like defile into that Breughelian lower world of wild and dream-like kirmessen (fairs); of charmed children playing their unending, timeless games; the peasant falling between two stools, the ass starving while regarding two discrete piles of hay, and in that same very crowded painting of proverbs personified, an immemorial peasant is pissing for the moon; taverns of oddest shape and lunatic form with wry, absurd, and arcane signboards abound. The people in these paintings and others are dancing, cavorting, skating, mooning, loitering, sleeping, working, dreaming, building, kissing, hugging, coupling, stalking, praising, praying, hunting, sowing, reaping; nothing human was alien to Pieter Breughel I. The returning hunters are forever poised against the snow, over the hill, down the declivity and into town, their hounds following, trailing their tails behind them: the hockey game is in progress on the frozen river, elsewhere a pig is being singed into deliciousness on a spit, a peasant woman is carrying a bundle of faggots across the bridge and the ravens speckle the white, swaddled, snowy winter scene. And the ferocious tumult attending the building of the Tower of Babel; that painting is a veritable directory of building trades and crafts, with the specifics of bygone hoists and cranes and derricks, with renderings of late medieval cable, line, and pully, and tools for every imaginary masonry, and the scramble of workers, lifting and pulling and cutting and smashing, the tangle of frenetic activity, the frenzied rushing this way and that, the pushing and squealing, the cacophony, the babel of tongues that filled the clangorous air. There is a flotilla of small ships rushing about and filling the harbor, they are carrying materials for the heaven-scraping, God-confounding building. And Icarus flailing through the air, splashing unnoticed into the alien sea, the plash unheard for the pre-eminent ploughman's drive through sillion, and the sheep's bleating and the cuckoo's mighty and insistent call. And the mowers' post-prandial Flemish stupor in "The Corn Harvest" in which a peasant is spread into a schlarafenland torpor of deepest

126

sleep, the other harvesters making a work-person's fête-champetre in the numbed midday landscape. The sun, pervasive, flashing at us in the waves of ripened uncut corn. How we are induced into this peasant embrace of cycled growth and harvest, of earth's bounteous hot gifts and of her frigid dearths and decimations. Would it be delicious to sprawl with those peasants in those long yellow-toned tunnels of fructification? It is a scene of gratification, of peace, of plenty, and overlaid with deep peasant content; the flocks of summer birds are concomitantly chattering in the heat-surfeited air. And those figures collapsed into drugged helplessness in "The Land of Cocayne", stretched into deepest lassitude, under that tree in that sweet but deadly never-never-land. And the bashful bride and near-hidden groom at their feast, merriment and solemnity are joined as the three-legged waiter helps carry in the wedding gruel. A set of the seasons peopled in pertinent occupation, dazzling for the depth and variety of activity, a jangle of Vivaldian accent and stroke, interrupted by sudden deep lyricisms, the larger compass of canvas broken into activities of quick hunting and slow fishing, and of constant planting, and tilling and reaping, and here and there the small glowing fires at which huddled peasants strain for a bit of warmth. And atypically a small painting, a portrait-like depiction of an old, possibly weary, but decidedly merry peasant, garbed in rude and colorful costume. The old man is trapped in far too small a space, he tends to heave, to crash against the picture's edges, as the frame struggles to hem him in; one does not know or remember any other portrait-like representation of peasants. One wonders at Breughel's intent! The limning and perpetuation of a specific face was a new-found aristocratic toy, not to be wasted on plebeians, boors, or rude persons generally. Is that perhaps why this old peasant is jammed into so tiny a space? One's head is filled with memories of Breughelian phantasies: the countless corpulent greasy fats combating the innumerable dessicated leans; battling themselves into oblivion in "The Fight between Carnival and Lent", and the terrorizing "Triumph of Death", in which Death's tireless, unceasing, continuous busy work is exemplified. We perceive Death as executioner, as reaper of lives in shipwrecks, fires, and other calamities, a veritable totentanz unfolds in a corner of the painting at the Prado; thus are cut down in neat

127

PB

hierarchical sequence; the Emperor, the Pope, the King, the Cardinal, et alia are all dealt the fatal knock, and here a death cart filled with skulls, pulled by a terrible flesh-losing nag, rumbles along, while many death figures toll the dull knolling bell of Death. A neo-Petrarchian Triumph of novel and vast proportions. But Pieter Breughel was no peasant, despite the assertive inventions of Karl van Mander, the northern Vasari. Breughel was friend to Ortelius and other humanists, he was acquainted with Coornheert, the engraver, scholar and master of Goltzius, and shared Coornheert's theism. Breughel was apparently one of the "Libertines" who placed themselves "above the individual confusions, and raised themselves to the apprehension of one truth common to all". Breughel made a transalpine trip to Italy in 1552 and that wonderful series of mountains and mountainous scenery testify to his long hours in the Alps: van Mander observed that "Breughel swallowed all the mountains and rocks and spat them out again after his return onto his canvases and panels."

Breughel. etching. 1964.

Georg Minne

Is it odd that Flanders, a fragment of European geography, should play so continuous and central a rôle in its artistic evolvement? Flanders, where the magical and bewitching method of painting with the oil medium was discovered and developed at the hands of van Eyck and Roger van der Weyden, Bosch and Breughel, Rubens and van Dyck, to note but the greatest luminaries; and on into the nineteenth century, miraculously, the tradition continued in "Les XX". Consider some of the artists, Ensor, Permecke, Meunier, Spillaert, Khnopf, Rops, van Russelberghe, et alia and the subject of this note and the accompanying wood-engraving, Georg Minne. Minne is unlike any other sculptor of the period: the swerving and curving fripperies and flippancies of Art Nouveau, endlessly damaging in other artists, grants him added means to achieve his most telling work: the kneeling youths, the blessés, and in many individual sculptures. His use of the Art Nouveau style is supremely personal and subtle in the extensions and retractions of swollen forms; he is sensitive in defusing the curvilinear; Minne is not a decorative sculptor and thus escapes the ravaging destructiveness of sinuosity; he is curt in his use of the mellifluous style. Minne's capital work is, no doubt, his ring of kneeling youths, seen to worst advantage in the immense Ghentian square that dwarfs and overwhelms it; that vast space crushes the figures into a reduction of themselves. Seen at the Folkgang Museum at Essen or the Kröller-Müller at Otterloo, the sculpture's scale becomes measurable, its meaning becomes perceivable. The harmonies that wend from figure to figure are near musical for subtlety of nuance and variation of mode: there is a quality in this work, which I can but dimly and I fear simplistically call religious; the kneeling as in genuflecting prayer, the self-embrace as though holding oneself *in* for God, the circle of figures forming a primordial ritual, the figures shedding a mutuality of interdependence and their stillness, retirement and deep inwardness. I know naught of Minne's religiosity except a host of his drawings of "The Pietà", oedipal, other-worldly, vaguely decadent, febrile, self-convoluting and fervid in the Virgin's clasping embrace of her very dead son. There is a hearkening towards Lehmbruck in "Le Petit Porteur des Reliquaire" in the solemnity of the figure, its rather attenuated torso and limbs, its tendency to absorb its surroundings. The "Wounded Ones" are sculptures of youths bending upwards in pain, firmly rooted, hands to head and face, the figures' fluidity broken by the angularities of elbows and knees; they are elegantly spasmodic. There are other sides to Minne's sculpture. Suffice, in this context, the virtues I allude to. And he made interesting and original woodcuts.

Minne. we. 1969.

Constantin Meunier

I am profoundly perplexed by aspects of Constantin Meunier's life and work. That perplexity is disturbing because I esteem Meunier as amongst the greatest of sculptors for his deep portrayal of the workers of his time and of his place. Georg Friederich Alexan, when he was not otherwise engaged in introducing a generation of American artists and others to the works of Kollwitz, Barlach, Beckmann, et alia, at his remarkable Tribune Subway Gallery, used to ask, Why is the clown the tragic personage so continually portrayed in nineteenth- and twentieth-century art? And he would answer his intriguing question as follows: No one is responsible for Pagliacci's or any clown's terrible plight. No one has been forced to become a clown. The clown as clown belongs to no class, no one can be held accountable for his dire necessity to be publicly mirthful while his heart cracks within. Thus a déclassé figure is to hand, profoundly unhappy, but not pointing with palsied hand at the guilty ones; the ones who have forced them into this pernicious rôle. Alexan would further demand of his quite alarmed and astonished listeners, Why weren't there artists ready to portray the nineteenth century's truly tragic figure? The proletarian, locked into satanic mills, worked endless hours in cruel circumstances and conditions, for dishonorable wages, ergo forced to inhabit dreadful urban slums, Glaswegian or Chicagoan, all the same. Why indeed were there no painters and sculptors ready for this task? The answer is, I fear, obvious. Artists and the proletarians labored for essentially the same persons and however vulgar this reasoning may be, I think it holds a kernel of truth, that begins to explain why there are so pitifully few depictions of Blake's and reality's satanic mills. I can only think of three portrayals of great industrial scenes: the most convincing is Menzel's painting of an "Iron and Steel Works", a vital representation of the sooty, sweaty, clangorous, dangerous, world: William Bell Scott, a lesser pre-Raphaelite, a poor poet and an unachieved painter, rises to his theme and in "Iron and Coal", 1855–60, paints the frenzied intensity of an open-shedded mill, near the wharves, making visible the hustling turmoil of Victorian industrialism: John Ferguson Weir, an American artist of great unfulfilled promise, painted at least two paintings, "The Iron

Foundry" and "Forging the Shaft", of the interior of the mill which cast the largest cannon of the American Civil War, the murderous Parrott guns of Melville's poem. J. T. Flexner says of Weir's "The Gun Foundry", "The finished painting shows a vast, crannied, dusty hall lit by flaming metal that flows from a tremendous cauldron into a huge mold. Machinery and workmen are everywhere . . . . Surprisingly the mood is altogether romantic. We seem to be not in a foundry watching the manufacture of a killer of men but rather in the bowels of the earth, where the very life force of Nature is being stoked by Wagnerian gnomes." "Forging the Shaft" tends to romanticize the mill in just the same way. A related painting picturing the workers outside of their factory is T. Anshutz's "Steelworkers' Noon Time", which is a tangential member of this tiny company of industrial painting: pictures that look into the overwhelming, the burgeoning, the consumptive presence of factories. There were artists who were socialists and anarchists struggling to ameliorate the near servitude of nineteenth-century workers, but their works of art do not come to palpable grips with the workers' reality. Courbet the Communard is an essentially rural painter; his worker crushes rocks in the countryside, his crucial socialist thinker, Proudhon, sits out of doors. Daumier is humanely sympathetic to all human beings, loves saltimbanques and mountebanks and the people of the street. He paints the occasional lonely, obviously oppressed, laundry woman but I know no painting of actual proletarians or their workplaces by him. One could, if the purpose of this short essay was a consideration of this fascinating and difficult subject, discuss the meager contribution to this iconography by van Gogh, Ford Maddox Brown, Munch and, much more directly than any of these, the lithographs by Theodore Steinlin for the "Assiette au Beurre" which depict the ravages of capitalism on its working people. It is beguiling to speculate as to why there were no pictorial equivalents to Dickens and of Mrs Gaskell, to Hugo and Zola. Is it that writing is temporal and painting spatial? As concerns subject those differences seem irrelevant. Both activities are geared to the same societal and personal impulses. So dear a committed socialist as Camille Pissarro was entirely content to paint peasants and an occasional factory pleasantly seen in retinal irrelevancy across a river, without stench, and as noiseless as one of

Meunier. etching [touched]. 1969.

134

his deep countryside scapes. Only two sculptors of greatness assayed the task and they are Constantin Meunier and Jules Dalou. Dalou like Courbet mounted the barricades and was exiled when the Commune was crushed. With the considerable help of Alphonse Legros he went to London and ultimately became a British citizen. A great sculptor but, despite his many exceptional and beautiful and pertinent works, not the subject of these words. It is perhaps interesting to note that Alexandre Charpentier, who along with Saint-Gaudens was the nineteenth century's greatest modeler in low relief, made portrait placques of Meunier and of Dalou. Meunier sees the noble qualities of the proletarian. He does on occasion depict workers treading in the postures of exhaustion, from the coal mines, but typically his worker rests from labor, is posed as Professor S. Kaplan has suggested, in a kind of Platonic ideal of labour. The Antwerp longshoreman in a Donatelloesque pose of easy relaxation stands with his hand on his hip, exceedingly casual, but infused with Quattrocento qualities of monumentality. What is crucial about Meunier is that all of his proletarians are conceived as heroic, and fitted out with the reaffirming strengths, the enlarging energies, the enduring largeness, of monumentality. Meunier does not make sculptures of the wretched of the earth; his proletarians contain and reaffirm their power. As though drawn from a new matrix, there is a prescience in these upstanding miners, a seeming knowledge of their futurity in the nobility of steelworkers. Was Meunier postulating a proletarian of a Utopian future? His figures are entirely free of the squalid circumstances that decimated and disfigured their existence. I am, alas, ignorant of Meunier's biography, and of the divers degrees of his successes, but I would postulate that it was his workers' unnaturalness, their being cast into stances of dignity and of powerful ease, that granted him the success he won. He was a regular exhibitor at the great French salons, was a cardinal and crucial influence on Rodin. Meunier had a very large exhibition in New York, where Columbia University bought a cast of his huge "Le Marteleur" to stand outside its engineering or metallurgy building, which I used to gawk at in late adolescent awe: that great sculpture is still awesome. I would like to unravel certain mysteries anent Meunier; I am perplexed by this master – but they are mysteries that perhaps issue from my

135

ignorance. Was he a socialist? What was the driving necessity that rendered proletarian figures the central subject of his sculpture and paintings and prints? There is a museum in Brussels dedicated to Constantin Meunier filled with paintings, drawings, prints, bronzes, and marbles; I have never visited it. Meunier was a member of that extraordinary group "Les XX" and exhibited with them. What were his relationships to Ensor? to Minne?, was he influenced by Emile Verhaereen? He stands apart from his time of sculptural ineptitude, of decorative fripperies, and endless ornamental flippancies, of the alienated absurdities of attenuated Art Nouveau. Meunier is in splendid isolation as the sculptor who invests the proletarian workers with the stance, the gesture, the attitude of monumentality.

Goltzius. woodcut. 1962.

Hendrik Goltzius

Hendrik Goltzius is the supreme Haarlem Mannerist; the arch disciple of Mad Rudolph's uniquely-visioned Bartolomeus Spranger. Goltzius was the progenitor of a brilliant school of engravers, with the luminous names of de Gheyn, Mathem, Saenredam, working after his designs and inventions. There is in Goltzius an abundance of exaggeration, an aggregation of gesture, an abandon of spirited prancing, an exhilaration of posing in serpentine stances, all excessive in Mannerist frenzy. But Goltzius is a draughtsman of stunning acuity, his work is consistently convincing because of the exquisite certainty of his drawing, of its consummate skill. However absurd or excessive the disposition of the figures, however contorted or distorted in mannered bending, twisting, reaching or tensing, they are not ludicrous because they are achieved with an absolute rightness and justness of means. Goltzius made a great many drawings and of all sorts. There are finished, fully realized drawings, conceived and executed with no other frame of reference than their own dazzling virtuosity and self-conscious beauty. And there are works done during his Italian wander-years: red and black chalk drawings of antique statuary and architecture; dynamic and intense portrait drawings; landscapes of alps and of lowlands, the drawings of mountains reminiscent of Breughel's crucial alpinescapes for their breadth of vision and incisiveness of observation; and many Ovidian themes, a specialty of the Haarlem school. Goltzius's depictions of antique divinities constitute a graphic theogony; and drawings of religious subjects, events and scenes from both Testaments, series of the Passion, of saints and martyrs. The subjects of his engravings are naturally enough directly related to his drawings. Goltzius overcame the limitations imposed by an accident which crippled his working hand (revealed to us in two exquisite drawings of that hand) to become one of the greatest masters of copper-engraving, a veritable wizard of the burin, capable of the subtlest, gentlest, most silvery effects and powerful, deep-black bravura engraving. The range and reach of his engraving is overwhelming, for they touch, reveal, comment on, are attentive to all later sixteenth-century humanistic and artistic interests and involvements. Early in his career, he engraved a

"Pietà", to demonstrate his vast skills, to declare his parity with the great Dürer. Goltzius's "Pietà" personifies virtuosity; it is Dürer's equal in technical expertness. Goltzius produced a lifetime full of engravings of superlative quality, tenebrously violent in the sudden sharp juxtapositions of white and black, or of a whispering subtlety in delineating an old and gnarled hand, or in depicting the stiff complexities of a linen ruff. How strident his standard-bearers are, with varieties of costume, caught in dappled patterns, glossy in silk or fur, resplendent in sun-reflecting armor. He engraved several inordinately large plates, my favorite being "The Midas Judgement", that distressing story with its dispiriting ending, its false and unfair judgement of Marsyas, the better musician who dared to challenge Apollo to a contest. Was he doomed to lose? – because, despite his skills, he presumed too far, he aspired too high; or was he foredoomed, was he condemned by the hubristic act of mastering Pan's thrown-away Syrinx, a gift to him from Juno, and no plaything for a demi-being of the likes of the faun Marsyas? Midas was dismissed with a new god-given set of ass's ears for preferring the superb magic of Marsyas's music. The magical duel took place before a new judge with the frightening interdictive example of his predecessor brightly and clearly before him – Apollo, of course, the finer musician, and Marsyas, poor upstart Marsyas, string him up, and skin him alive. Goltzius devises a kind of fête champetre in which the muses disport in elegant reclinings, while Apollo plays his ur-fiddle before the judge, like a primordial Paganini at center-stage, while to the right, Midas, Marsyas and other satyrs attend the scene. The five large prints known as the "Masterworks" are bravura works, tours-de-force, deliberately engraved in the manners of Dürer, Lucas Barocci, et al.; extravagant but unlovely works. The portrait drawings and engravings by Goltzius are of these kinds: a series of very small but intensively perceived portraits, virtual miniatures, but free of the miniaturist's diminishing, surface-loving, vignette-tending propensities, they are decidedly not the work of a miniaturist; Goltzius vests the tiniest, the most gem-like portrayal, with his wider vision. They loom large, these portraits, and project personality. As we examine them closely and wonder at their strong, delicate minusculaties, we ponder the intricate means of their facture. There are small engravings in silver and gold

138

Goltzius. etching. 1962.

meant to be worn as pendants. Robert, Earl of Leicester is one of these; proofs were taken with the lettering reversed. And there are monumental portrait drawings of artists, done while on his Italian trip, Giovanni Bologna, Taddeo Zuccaro, Francavilla et alia in dashing, revelatory black and red chalk; the artists are laid open to our deepening stare, they flash from the sheet with the vividness of the quick. These portrait drawings astonish me for their immediacy, and for the power of their expression of affect; once seen, one's image of these persons is forever fixed. The large engraving of his master, the complex, many-sided Coornheert, stands with those masterworking depictions of inevitability, Holbein's "Erasmus", Lucas's "Maximillian", Dürer's "Pirckheimer", Rembrandt's "De Jonghe"; unalterable works, their perfections are immutable. The final state of the Coornheert displays his attributes in the surrounding margins, cascades of fluttering books, artificers' instruments and tools, a stack of weapons, palettes and brushes, bespeak his diverse accomplishments. The great face looms out of its oval concavity, broad-headed, hard-staring, evoking this serious artist, teacher and writer. But within the layers of Goltzius's variegated graphic oeuvre, I cherish most the chiaroscuros. The color-printed woodcuts by Goltzius are virtually unlike all others because of the manifest lack of the intervening hand of the professional woodcutter, the formschneider. That dull hand stultifies because it inevitably imposes the deadness, the sterility, the lifelessness of the mechanical executor. It is the interposition of technique without intention. The motivating force of the work has been throttled. Late in the fifteenth century and early in the sixteenth, the formschneider rendering the works of Dürer and Altdorfer, for instance, had achieved unbelievable feats of cutting, (Thomas Bewick, in disbelief, posited the notion of two blocks to explain the remarkable effects of crosshatching; a canny idea, but not credible as cut blocks exist, with the wizard-like cutting intact). It is the brilliance of the draughtsmanship, so hotly, so quickly, so passionately relayed from brain to hand, from hand to block, from block to paper, that makes Goltzius's involvement with and commitment to the cutting a necessary concomitant to their creation; this notion is reinforced by the delineative inevitability and autographic authority of this late chiaroscuro flowering. It was the

140

sparking of a near dead medium into late luminance. The subjects of Goltzius's twenty-odd woodcuts are akin to the themes in his other prints. What impelled him into the woodcut? Surely it is the greater strength inherent in the rather coarse-cut lines; thus there's a directness, a simplification of means, an immediacy of expression; the four small Virgilian landscapes and the larger "Arcadian Landscape" have a freshness of impact, especially when proofed on deep blue paper and heightened with hand-applied white. My favorite Goltzius chiaroscuro is "Pluto", one of a series of Antique gods. The protean ruler god of the underworld is outlined against a background of roaring chaos, of conflict and of conflagration. The mighty figure, seen from behind, with arms and legs spread as though set to embrace the artfully dimmed scenes of devastation that ensue at his behest; there is protean energy in the robust stance. The figure massively fills the oval that holds it, the god stands sprung as though wrought in steel, a figure without compassion and pity, posturing with an inhuman gesture of overwhelming hubris. The work is achieved with all of Goltzius's accustomed sureness of articulate portrayal, with that deftness, that persuasive totality of control of the great master.

Jacob de Gheyn II

There were three Jacob de Gheyns. They were successive. The progenitor, the grandfather of the third, is a dim figure who is of little interest. His grandson worked in the magically umbrageous manner of Hendrick Terbruggen; his figures of philosophers and martyrs sit in isolation; apparently consumed by their own gigantic cast shadows. I know his engravings only: his later history is somewhat odd. I have a memory of reading of his suffering deeply, perhaps dying, in a heretical delusion. It is his father Jacob de Gheyn II, the prodigious draughtsman, who has trapped my astonished attention. De Gheyn's range of interest seems limitless; of him one recites the Roman maxim, "Nothing human is alien to me." A member of Goltzius's inner circle, his mastery of the drawing media is staggering for its consummacy, for its perfections, for its sheer linear beauties. De Gheyn's drawings entrance us for the felicitous ease of their unfolding, their towering strengths, the dear wit of their minute observations, their grandeur, their might and majesty, their inventive variousness, their grace and their wizardry, their startling inventiveness and their magical propensities. De Gheyn's diversity is vast. Has anyone ever drawn a mouse with greater tenderness or sharper acuity? The mice in that Amsterdam (Rijksmuseum) drawing seem to be all aquiver with their sniffing, shivering, darting reality preserved, indeed heightened. And the drawing of three flies at Frankfurt a/M, – how they seem to barely touch the paper, how their unheard buzz is surprising, how incredible the skill that thus captures their evanescent dipteral actuality. And the lizard also at Frankfurt, one can only think to compare it to one of Jamnitzer's lizards, but the Jamnitzer is cast from nature (Naturselbabguss), de Gheyn's ingenious eye has trapped onto vellum the vivid twisting and thrashing about of the creature. His drawings of frogs never hop very far from the memorized layers that border the pool of our imagination. They spark from their sheets with a jocund ease: they do splits and acrobatics, they imitate humans, they strut like prebenders, they gape, they are unblinkingly pompous. The delicious de Gheyn frogs dance, they play instruments, viols of course – do they read and write books as well? They are so convincingly drawn, conceived with such verve, with that "crackerjack" virtuosity,

142

De Gheyn. woodcut. 1967.

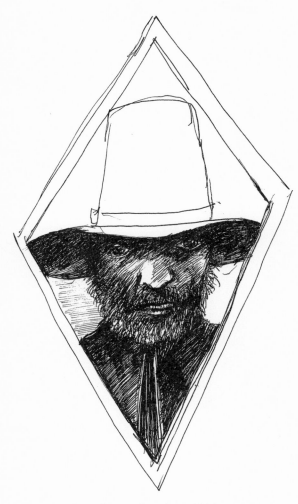

De Gheyn. drawing. 1986.

which electrically charge de Gheyn's drawings. His tiniest drawings bristle with tenacious liveliness, and his immensely large drawings of witches' sabbaths are all abustle with wild scenes of hexen transformation, witches cavorting and tumbling and flying in the huge cavern spaces of the walpurgis night. In the wondrous multi-leveled scene of the "Preparation for the Sabbath" (Berlin) the hot stink of witchery stirs us as with a propulsing blast, a hex disappears up a chimney, acrid smoke fills the scene in which demons and witches consult the occult tomes, frogs and skulls abound, novitiates are led in from the right, and in the center a great libationary pot of the devil-knows-what is boiling and throwing up plumes of smoke and vapor in which can be seen a witch riding a goat or a devil astride a bull. The scene is very scenographic, with action on at least three levels, with space piercing arches, overmantling chimney pieces and a cut-away at center to a scene in a cellar, a figure under a spell, while cats scamper about, toying with long-tailed rats. How one would wish it all to come to life with a Mozartian blast and go forward in da Pontian liveliness. In an even more theatrical drawing, "Witches' Sabbath" (Ashmolean, Oxford) the scene is revealed through a great moss-hung stone arch. Employing motifs from the alchemist's study, the anatomist's theater and the Sabbath, the drawing with its ominous and immense cast shadows give pause, indeed it is quite scary. A male figure, lying back with arm flung out, has his thorax excavated, one leg is bizarrely up, a frog pinned in dissection is next to him. Looming over him is seen the head and neck of a skeletal horse, and at his head a witch studies a large tome in deep absorption. Cats and mice are everywhere. At the center right of the drawing one seated and one standing witch are deep in the "unlawful art" involving a cat and a small poupée of human aspect. The standing witch is pointing to the partially dissected cadaver; her figure and her pointing arm and hand are thrown in huge shadow against the back arched wall. A severed rotted head, a broomstick, vials and jars, bats and spumes of smoke pour into the scene from an invisible furnace. A weirdly beautiful and terrifying drawing. There is one other of these immense witch drawings at Oxford preserved with many other great drawings at Christ Church. It is in two halves and called "Preparation for the Sabbath": but I shall forswear the describing of it; instead I will compile a list and short

144

De Gheyn. drawing. 1986.

145

description of de Gheyn's divers subjects. Every human activity is fair game for his virtuoso pen and brush: see "Cavalry Charge" (Rotterdam), full of the clang and blast of trumpets, the clamor of war, the rising dust of battle: a winged demon with heavy dugs, thumbing her nose with both hands, very much the way I used to as a child, this "Fantastic Creature" (Brussels) has great vivacity and is completely believable. There are "Studies of Gypsies" (Chicago), winsome, sympathetic, part costume, part beguiling portrayals of children; "Study of Three Hags" (Haarlem), and "Study of Four Heads" (Haarlem), and "Study of Young Witches" (Paris) and "Study of Two Old Women" (Lugt, Paris) are piercing considerations of these various types, not in creating a typology of hags and witches but always these personages are freshly perceived. De Gheyn's drawings of the female nude are strikingly unlike those of his contemporaies: as Professor Judson observes in his book *The Drawings of Jacob de Gheyn*, ". . . his drawings of nudes which are absolutely different from those drawings by his contemporaries". Goltzius's are elegant and mannered while Abraham Bloemaert's are more idealized and sophisticated. De Gheyn for the first time since Albrecht Dürer studies the nude both for its perfections and imperfections and produces drawings that will only be rivaled by Rembrandt's 1658 etching of the "Negress Lying Down". His sublime drawings of the female nude, notably in the "Studies of Four Women at Their Toilet" (Brussels) is predictive of both Rubens and Rembrandt. Here are human beings, not a Raphaelesque ideal, with no Mannerist neurosis, but realized, fullbodied, with a perfected mingling of line and shade: the gesture of the toilette is natural, the implied space believable, the figures' physicality perfectly achieved. They do indeed adumbrate Rembrandt. To quote Judson again regarding the beautiful drawing of a "Sleeping Woman" (Brunswick), ". . . but de Gheyn's way of seeing and presenting the nude was revolutionary. Whereas Goltzius and his contemporaries drew nudes that were still based on the anti-Classical ideal, de Gheyn's 'Sleeping Woman' is a natural figure. De Gheyn does not draw a nude based upon an ideal, Classical or anti-Classical, but a living woman with all of her beauty and blemishes. She is not posed but drawn while actually asleep and de Gheyn not only achieves a sense of a resting form surrounded by bed clothes but . . . suggests the atmosphere of the bedroom." That black sleeping woman is suffused with the reality of deep sleep, in repose, calm, utterly still and very beautiful. I shall not go on listing *all* the categories of de Gheyn's drawings, but any consideration of de Gheyn's drawing must perforce include his drawings of landscape which are an extension of Goltzius's landscape visions, as they move away from the alpine phantasies of Breughel toward a world perceived in its real dimension and proportion. As Judson observes, "This new trend appears first in J. de Gheyn's 1602 'Study of Fishermen on the Beach' . . . the composition is not idealized; in its spread-out arrangements, with no central point of concentration . . . ." It is interesting to see de Gheyn develop from the making of brilliant drawings of landscape, heavily influenced by Breughel, Paul Bril and his master Goltzius; the landscapes ease away from the tumult of ravines and mountains, from steep cliffs, arches and long distant views, the surface all astir with scintillating, short strokes, to views of farmyard, sea-coast and even large landscaped vistas replete with robbers and other actors. One does not move from Bril to Rembrandt in one breathtaking leap; instead one must trek through a landscape but slowly perceived to be changing, and Jacob de Gheyn's mature drawings are marking-stones denoting the ongoing passage from the visionary and the haunted to the perceptible and the actual. Along with those ingenious frogs my memory holds in immutable clarity de Gheyn's portrait, both drawn and engraved of Tycho Brahe, the Danish astronomer; which brings me to near the end of this brief scan of de Gheyn's activity as a draughtsman, wanting only a mention of his superb portrait drawings. It is hardly surprising to discover that his portraits form another recognizable component in the totality of his oeuvre. The powerful drawing, "Young Artist Seated at a Table" (Yale University, New Haven) is, I am certain, a portrait of Jacob III: at a table strewn with inkpots and pens, the young artist looks up, as at an interruption, he regards the intruder with an intense quizzical look, his raised right hand heightening the questioning response; a delightful rendering of a bright, impudent son reacting to another of father's incessant interruptions. The drawing is achieved in de Gheyn's most direct, most incisive manner; the strokes of the pen explode onto the paper with a life-enhancing vitality. And there are other admirable portrait drawings expressive in their various ways, the interests, the developments, the unfolding of de Gheyn's life as an artist straying from the depths of Haarlem Mannerism to the broad humanistic plateau, reinforced with conceptions of the natural world influenced by Leonardo and by Dürer, and driving on toward Rembrandt, who is the fulfillment of many of de Gheyn's indications.

De Gheyn. etching. [detail]. 1962.

Hercules Seghers

Hercules Seghers's hallucinated vision is not readily explicated. Some thrust him on a Breughellian Alpine trip, that he never took; others have him all adaze in the Dutch hilly province of Arnheim, thinking that he could mistake those gentle hills for a Himalayan range; to no avail. The mountains that Seghers etched rear up tumultuous and cavernous only in the illusory geography of his brain. The sides of the rent mountains are strewn with an avalanche of stones, heaped all about, pellmell, in proliferated disorder; or towering to peaks, heaving volcanic eructations, massive up-building eruptions; the wild inventing of a mad flatlander. The rocks coruscate in Seghers's dusk-haunted, deep-toned prints. The hues in printed color resonate differently than in painted color, they vibrate with an uncomplicated clarity; there is a simpler purity in the interacting tones and in their relationships: printed colors resound, amplify, are crushed into the very fabric at the paper and meld under the enormous pressure of an etching press into a fusion that is unachievable with paint and brush. What is arresting and very surprising is that prior to Seghers's imaginative explorations there is no printed color from metal plates, even though the art of chiaroscuro or the printing of colored images from a series of wood blocks had long been known and was highly developed. To achieve the novel and original effects his ardent phantasy demanded, his technical facility was driven to feats of stupefying inventiveness. He stained and painted parts of papers and linens before printing; he inked his etched copperplates in one or two colors other than those used in the prepared papers and cloths; and, finishing the work with further in-painting, accomplished in the process works of startling new facture and aspect. He produced tonal effects akin to aquatint by lightly scratching close parallel lines into the polished surface of the refractory copperplate; he devised a method of inverting tonalities, compounding figure and ground and at times attaining the odd perplexities of photographic negatives. The images that Seghers invented are always surprising and his etchings of trees are spectral and haunted: they climb upward in broad jagged leaps, or crunch their slow, indomitable march, displaying time's decorations, the scars and wounds of committed upward passage. One of his trees

Seghers. etching [unpublished]. 1954.

149

seems to fling itself ever upwards, bearing on its flag-like limbs a ganglion downfall of Spanish moss, printed and painted in Far-Eastern-like mysterious tones of orange-tinged reds and ochre-ridden greens. I remember being struck with stunning unexpectedness when first seeing that print projected on a New School classroom wall; I thought it not credible that this masterwork was the issue of the seventeenth century. Seghers etched two small "Tempests"; both have a tiny submerged near-lost ship, making haphazard way in tempestuous, raging, roaring and whelming seas; one print is awash in grey and green browns, the other in deepest, tortuous, frightening black-blues. These two small etchings of heaving seas are like the mountains, convulsant, seething and turbulent. Seghers's life is wonderfully obscure and his history is replete with myth and legend: that he used up, it is said, all the family linen, madly printing his etchings; that he was a drunkard; that he fell down the stairs of his house and broke his neck, all in a drunken stupor; and other nonsensical tales of this magical Haarlem artist. Rembrandt the zealous collector owned seven paintings by Hercules Seghers and several of his copperplates; indeed, he ruined one copper by scraping and burnishing away the figures of Tobias and of Raphael the angel, and substituting the Holy Family fleeing into Egypt; but so deep was Rembrandt's respect for Seghers that he left the beautiful Eschelonian landscape unaltered; one can still find traces of Raphael's wings in the newer Rembrandtian context. Seghers's prints are uncommonly rare; the flat lowlanders of his day were content with the landscape they could see, they had no interest in what they must have counted as Seghers's visual ravings, they abjured his prints; they can now be seen, radiant, glorious and unique in the print cabinet of the Rijksmuseum of Amsterdam.

150

Seghers. etching. 1962.

Rembrandt

It is cretinous, I readily admit, to count artists as the five greatest, to stupidly compose lists of the mightiest paintings (as though they were in contention), to inanely assert the primacy of this over that, to declare on the world's air waves which five discs and which three books you would require on your desert isle, excluding the Bible and Shakespeare; it is indeed simple-minded in the extreme, but of universal practice. Thus your indulgence is urged, to permit me to place the following nonsense before you. Which of the following five artists do you revere the most? Michelangelo, Raphael, Leonardo, Dürer, Rembrandt? Stay, consider and choose: Rembrandt is my overwhelming first choice. Not to deny the others, only to extoll Rembrandt for his incredible penetràtion to the hot core of our essential humanness. Leonardo penetrated to the knowledge of the knowable but his art did not unbolt the successive gates that keep hidden the seat of the human soul; Rembrandt's did. Michelangelo scoured the human figure to render delineative reality to its diverse and precious precincts, but his art did not throw open the terraces of human psychology; Rembrandt's did. Dürer made viable and perceptible the multifarious personages of theology, but his art did not pierce the skeins that entail human frailty; Rembrandt's did. Raphael was an orchestrator of figures perambulating the spaces of the Athens School, but his art did not betray the source of human love; Rembrandt's did. Rembrandt crashed into the unreachable matrix of our humanity, to where no painter had trespassed before him. It is Rembrandt's passion for "alles menschlich" that isolates him, ennobles him, endears him. All great artists are singular in their genius, in the particularities of their sensibilities, in the uniqueness of their voices, but no artist before Rembrandt and but few that followed him were so trenchant in their preoccupation with the human psyche. Thus the well-established art of portraiture is lifted to a new and novel purpose; beyond the perpetuative tracery of specific features we see laid open the sitters' psychological being. Rembrandt sends shafts of illuminative brilliance deep into the characters of his sitters. He sets them into half-lights, clear and hidden away by depths of lights and shadows, with all shrouding and enveloping mysteries of penumbral interweavings of massed densities of greys, gaining in intensity, deepening in hue; it is secretive display, the candid folded into the covert. It is as though the greatest prestidigitator of all time had only blackness and whiteness to deploy in his magic and is able to recreate reality with those limited means. Rembrandt sends his sitters' eyes into backward piercing looks, revealing the fonts of personality. Rembrandt dapples humanity in that quivering light of gold. The persons in Rembrandt's painted world stare through layers of glazed and scumbled light, raveled in silver-edged shades. Rembrandt's atmosphere is concocted out of enlightened darknesses; his blacks are revelatory transparencies, our gaze passes through his shadows: Rembrandt is never obscure. The silvered gold that cascades over Rembrandt's people is nascent like the sun, it reveals them whole, inside and out, a new formulation, a configuration of lights flashing in darks that is novel to our firmament. Rembrandt *is* a constellation, *his* superabundance of form-making energy gleams with endless vigor through time. Rembrandt was, of course, a very successful, cosmopolitan painter, fluent in the usages of the tough, competitive professional Amsterdam Guild of St Luke. He painted to the tastes and desires of his patrons, helped them form those tastes and desires, and Dryden's wry observation about Peter Lely is applicable to Rembrandt: "That although they were all like one another . . . they were not like their sitters; because he always studied himself more than those that sat to him." What was there about his face that so continuously absorbed and arrested his intensest notice? It was singularly his and his alone, to arrange and rearrange till the end of his time. In the private recesses of his studio Rembrandt was free of the tiresome demands of a Rokin herring dealer, for more light and less gloom, more color and less shadow, more order and less dissolution. He was free in his closet, free from the demands of the anticipated, the expected, the average, the commonplace, the unadventurous. Alone in his workroom he could regard the conglomerate totality of his boorish features, his great potato of a nose, and those two dark, round, unyielding eyes set into a face, the skin of which assumes the pallid pallor of the atelier and again, oddly, flushed with rude ruddiness. No, it was not the particularities of his face, but the miraculous capacity of every human face to reveal the entire range of discoverable expressiveness that entranced him. How

153

Rembrandt. etching. 1963.

avidly Rembrandt play-acts before his mirror; how pliable his sweet-homely face as he laughs uproariously, or grins, or grimaces, or leers, or wraps his visage in a sly, even shy smile. The works are infused with that special species of honesty, the probity that only flows from total privacy, from that self-confrontation in the mirror. We all play out our phantasies before that magical silvered piece of glass. See how the young Rembrandt in an ongoing series of paintings, drawings and etchings portrays the mimetic posturings, here pop-eyed in surprise, and there, eyes popping in presumed terror. He shows himself in the raggedy clothes of a beggar or in a velvet cap, deep in contemplative mien. He painted himself three times with abundant curly hair, looking in startled wonder at the world about him; the light crushing into golden crystals against his head. And in work after prodigious work Rembrandt shines the revelatory light at and into himself. Now he is the middle-aged grave philosopher, struggling through the gloom of a deep speculation, and then he is in plumed helm, a warrior rushing into the light. Rembrandt was a spendthrift; he squandered fortunes on paintings and sculpture, drawings and prints, medals and ojects du vertu, armor and stuffs from the East and West, embroidered or threaded in gold and silver, tapestries, silks, brocades and velvets, with which to bedeck himself and his models, transforming a Singel tramp into the faded and bemused King Saul and a lad from the Grachts into the aspiring David. How he loved to don this array of finery, helmets and breastplates, turbans and hats of every description. Indeed, some time in late youth Rembrandt puts on a hat and the rich crop of curly hair is never seen again; that and other hats are pulled tight against those straying curls and he never shows himself bareheaded thereafter (with the exception of one small drawing). I must own to speculating about this odd hirsute withdrawal and offer this musing: all the syndics, and all the doctors and magisters, and virtually all the males Rembrandt portrayed, are wearing hats. Rembrandt may suddenly have gone bald, but I rather think he was asserting his maturity, of attaining his mastery of achieving artistic (painterly) respectability. Once he felt entitled to that hat he plunked it down and never took it off: how could he resist the rich and abundant downfalling of sonorous shadows that are cast by the great brims of Dutch seventeenth-century hats? The self-portraits

155

continue throughout all the years of Rembrandt's life. They grow larger and broader and deeper, they are profoundly solemn, they laugh, they inquire, they squawk, and they brood, like hulking monoliths pondering the nature of life, of reality, of death. But this endless self-portrayal had the further purpose of allowing Rembrandt a proving ground in which he could experiment, to invent and discover new means, to calibrate (subjectively) the value of innovative deployments. His purpose was to extend the range in the pictorial explication of character and personality. Rembrandt had many students and followers; the very best work close to his manner, but a chasm separates their efforts, splendid though they may be, from his. One cannot confuse Bol, Dou, Flinck, Ovens, Eeckhout, et al., with Rembrandt; one cannot mistake their deliciously warming fires for the searing, scalding, scarifying furnaces of Rembrandt. An Aert de Gelder seemed touched by that same muse of sweet-tempered humanity, but he lacked the inventiveness, the depth, the towering reach; a Carel Fabritius seemed branded with a similar brilliance, but that wondrous gift and that very young life were squandered when a mint exploded. Rembrandt in the sublime manner of the great was on inevitable occasions weaker and something less than glorious; we must be aware of the betraying humanness in even the most titanic of artists, that they cannot only work at the high-mark of their genius; they will and they do falter. Some idiot art-historians propose to create a canon of acceptable works out of only the highest levels of achievement. Within the capacity of an artist to create in a protean way is vested that artist's necessity to be clumsy, hapless, inept, and mediocre. That duality is central in all human creativity. One watches with continuous amusement as the Rembrandt canon is reduced to naught by van Dyck, dangerously swelled by Bredius, and brutally cut back by Gerson. We must perforce accept the ever-burgeoning grandeur of a Shakespeare, a Michelangelo, a Bach and a Rembrandt. The immensity of their greatness curdles our belief and defies our understanding. What is surprising and distressing is how much *like* them their *best* contemporaries are, but the titans are colossally expanded and extended by small but crucial differences: the far deeper thrust, the farther quest, the broader concern, the profounder insight, the *in*capacity for compromise and accommodation, the puissant straining,

156

the over-weening certainty, the interconnecting arches, the multi-levels of meaning, the enriching ambiguities, the tumult of energy and the unassuageable desire. Artists like Rembrandt and those of his precious confraternity contrive to sustain and deploy all of these qualities with their immeasurable natural gifts, their confident diligence, and continuous industry. It entirely suits our stereotypical conception of the neglected and starving artist to have Rembrandt toppled from his high pedestal of esteem, power and wealth into those penurious stalls reserved for so-called genius misunderstood and trammeled. The instance of Vincent van Gogh is constantly before us. The dire and stupefying and total rejection of van Gogh's work has robbed us of critical certainty, and provides us with an abiding false image of the artist, a genius or otherwise, rotting from vilifying uninterest, gross indifference, the miseries of poverty and the calumny of misunderstood neglect. Most artists until the later eighteenth century were amply supported and consistently employed by ecclesiastical and royal patronage. The loss of churchly and princely patronage somewhat imperiled the artist, but the inrushing merchants, capitalists and bourgeoisie soon happily replaced the earlier patrons. There were casualties, but this is not the place to discuss the emergence of works of art as commodities, subject to taste, the vagaries of fashion, the uncertainties of the marketplace and the ongoing fluctuations of these. Rembrandt was, perhaps, too obsessed with beams of light and the delicious disorder of artificial light piercing the darkness at several simultaneous points. His work became too awesomely personal, pushing beyond the accepted modalities of a van der Aelst; it was indeed caviar for the general; but the pertinacious never abandoned him. Rembrandt's deep trouble was with creditors, and his bankruptcy the issue of his reckless extravagances in acquiring works of art. So massive was the glut of collected goods that the auctioneers, to use their parlance, had recourse to "lotting up" parcels of drawings and prints. It is presumed knowledge that Rembrandt owned seven paintings by Hercules Seghers, two of his copper-plates. And what of Seghers's wondrous etchings? He owned at least one Mantegna drawing: did he have others? And Mantegna's prints and his followers'? If only we could untie those bundles of prints and drawings and pick them over, uncovering Rembrandt's predilections,

Rembrandt. drawing. 1987.

and learn the close details of all the paintings, and sculptures, and medals, etc., that were sold: that is but an art-historian's pipe-dream. Rembrandt's son Titus and his companion-wife Hendrijke Stoffels set up a painting business with Rembrandt as a principal in the "maatschappij". He was forced to leave his grand house, but the vision of him fallen into the Amsterdamian stews or obscured in the dregs of the Amsterdamian backwaters is false. Charles Laughton playing Rembrandt was grand in rags, and histrionically articulate as a pauper, while the veritable Rembrandt was receiving commissions from as far away as Sicily. We love Rembrandt. His Promethean works do not reduce us to exclamatory wonder, to expressions of disbelief and awe. Or, if we do respond with marvel at his works, these responses have compacted into them elements of affection and regard that are generally absent in responses to paintings of other titans. The mature Rembrandt does not posture, he is not outlandish in gesture, he does not, to use Eakins's phrase in re Rubens, requisition "the strength of a Hercules to wind up a little watch". He abjures the artificial and he has little recourse to fustian. The glory of his invention lies in his redefinition of the ordinary, his mighty monumentalization of the quotidian, the common, the unglorified. The deep amber that glows in Rembrandt entrances us. We relate to the people who inhabit his lambent spaces. His nude men and women are naked, are lifted out of no ideal mold; they are simulacra of ourselves, big-bellied and fat-assed, ponderous in overweight or angular in thinness, but believable as Danae or St Jerome or Bathsheba. His humans are stunningly frail and like us, as occasion demands, heroic; they enact in their quiet, deliberate and inevitable ways, all the states of our emotional scale. Thus Saskia is flirtatious in offering her floral virginity as "Flora", and stolidly statuesque as "Juno" surveying her husband's godly lack of control. How deeply bemused is King Saul and how easily deceived is the old, the blessing Isaac; and Christ's grief is palpable. I do not mean to sentimentalize Rembrandt. He is entirely free of sentimentality, or of any other falsehoods. His work is deeply beautiful because it is profoundly truthful. Rembrandt is accessible, but he is not homely, or cozy. Rembrandt's fulgency reveals the ache, the joy, the penetrating pain, the spreading gladness, the overhanging gloom, the surging goodness; he paints the entirety

159

of human experience. Rembrandt's paintings cleave to the heart and vest themselves in the brain. He moves us more trenchantly than any painter before or since.

Lievens. drawing. 1987.

Jan Lievens

Lievens had the titanic bad luck to enter into apprenticeship with
Pieter Lastman precisely when Rembrandt did; Lievens's lustre was
thereafter forever tarnished; no one could long stand against that
Rembrandtian dazzle. When they as celebrated wunderkinder were
still grinding color for Lastman, Lievens was counted as the more
gifted of the two, and was expected to achieve the palm, to reach
greater painterly levels; witness his early and wonderful "Raising of
Lazarus". It is universally asserted that Lievens lacked that staying
temper, that steely underpinning, that purposeful armature that grants
an artist the inner and outer strength to sustain the highest demands
of pictorial probity. Lievens, they say, was weak, his effort and
achievement faltered and as Rembrandt deepened his means and
vision, Lievens fell victim to the flesh-pots, his paintings assuming the
mien of a second-rank artist, but astonishingly Lievens made a series
of woodcuts which are that medium's last great historical
efflorescence. (Pace Zanetti. Pace Jackson.) During its greatest
moments at the hands of Dürer, Holbein, Amman and Stimmer, the
designing and cutting of woodcuts were separate functions – one
artistic, the other an act of artisanry (formschneider). It is likely that
Goltzius cut his woodcuts; there is no doubt that *only* Lievens's hand
could have given his woodcuts their immediacy, verve, spontaneity
and dynamism, that inevitable personal quality that bespeaks the
master's direct engagement. The remarkable, freely conceived woodcut
of a stump of trees pulsates with the vigor of one of his intense reed-
pen drawings: the freshness of vision preserved in a breathtakingly
original freshness of technique. The other woodcuts are of portrait-like
figures, disposed in chairs, brought close-up to us, one in the subtle
shades of chiaroscuro color, the other a tiny print of a philosopher, so
cunningly cut that it was long taken as a Rembrandt etching. These
entirely unexpected woodcuts delight us for the virtuoso-like
deployment of the woodcutter's knife and convince us by the achieved
space-displacing actuality of persons forever caught in space-resolved
compositions.

Maria Sibylla Merian

The rare union of genius and intrepidness is the key to the artistry
and personality of Maria Sibylla Merian. She had the temerity to
brave, accompanied by her young daughter and studio baggage, the
hostility, incivility and the purest, sheerest terror concurrent with a
seventeenth-century sea-voyage to the tropics. One can imagine the
passage of the powerful Frankfurt-born artist into the steaming
purlieus of Surinam. And how she searched every aspect of Surinam's
terrain, looking for insects and their host plants at the very white
overheated heart of the jungle; she probed into its deepest and most
hidden density of bush and forest, its misted overgrown and
overhung waterways, its vales and its hills. She scoured Surinam's
entire geography to find, to preserve and to delineate the variety of
insects and flowering plants that flourished within its boundaries.
What a display of concentrated effort and how brilliant the result. One
is tempted to assert that the profound difficulty of her task imparted a
qualitative leap toward the work's ultimate magnificence. Does the
deeper struggle against inordinate obstacles, beyond the real-enough
struggle to advance one's work from concept to actuality, does the
greater struggle bond the work with an otherwise absent felicitous
strength? I rather think it does and M. S. Merian's stunning books are
touched with the glowing fervor of that immense undertaking. The
pages of her *Metamorphosis Insectorum Surinamensium* are pellucidly
vibrant; they are all aglow in varied brilliancies of color, and how
bright the color still is, being hidden in light-denying closed books.
The insects, diverse in their morphological evolvements, are displayed
in a dazzle of painted hues and engraved lines. And beyond the glory
of the insects cavorting, slithering and creeping across their spaces on
those heat-stained pages, is their fixment into the plants on and in
which their existence is sustained. The book readily assumes its place
as a work of magnificence in the history of bookmaking. The
indomitable Maria Sibylla Merian brought home from Surinam
drawings and studies which she composed into the alluring
compositions that the professional engravers fixed into the dense and
mirror-like surfaces of copperplates; the resultant proofs were then
spread out on tables and watercolored based on a model she prepared

Merian. etching [touched detail]. 1969.

and one presumes carefully supervised. The book is very large, a large folio, and represents a massive expenditure of effort, time, and money. Of course, only a limited number of copies were produced; it is a difficult speculation to precisely determine the quantities made, probably something between two to three hundred copies . The book is extremely rare today. M. S. Merian is also the author of *Die Europaische Insekten*, a work of only slightly lesser originality when compared to the Surinam masterwork, but of an astonishing delicacy and gossamer-like evanescence, perceived and realized by Merian within the frame of those insects' reality. The heart of Maria Sibylla Merian's achievement was the pursuit of the radiant realism of insect, flower, and plant. Through the artistic devices at her command, through the usages of distortion, of color, of compositional originality, she reveals the transient stages of insectival metamorphoses in a new and breathtakingly beautiful way. Merian worked within a well-established tradition; there had been many a glorious folio of flower and plant life, and numerous large quartos dealing with natural history generally, with shells, and birds and animals and minerals. It is that her work is more profound, is touched by grandeur, pries deeper into the secret and mysteriously hidden life and ways of insects. Her work is entomologically paramount and has never been superseded. The Netherlandish burgeoning mercantilism with resultant attitudinal structures, within and without the studios, was obviously crucial in the development of the desire and demand that their works of art reveal the real world in all quotidian plainness and in all of its magical ordinariness. Those infantile capitalists caused the size of paintings to shrink, to take on the qualities of portable treasure. All within nature and in civilized life was of pictorial interest to these burghers; thus, inter alia, a tradition of subject painting, drawing and engraving developed within what used to be called "Natural History" and now denoted as the separate disciplines of Zoology, Botany, Entomology, etc. In M. S. Merian's time that tradition was quite well established, and being the daughter of Mathieu Merian and the wife of Molenaer, a painter, engraver and publisher, she was privy to the publishing strategems of the Kalverstraat, Amsterdam's version of the Parisian Rue St Jacques. Maria Sibylla Merian had a very clear perception of what was possible and likely and what was decidedly unlikely; she thus exploits her knowledge of the professional engravers' capacities and qualities and of their deficiencies and limitations. The glories and felicities of her published work shine in the perfection of her designs flawlessly engraved by the maleficent hack engravers, a remarkable instance of knowledge and control, overriding the deadening tendency of the translator.

Merian. drawing. 1986.

165

Romeyn de Hooghe

Otto Benesch, the cataloguer of Rembrandt's drawings, the pre-Hitlerian director of the Albertina, the author of one of the rare, because of its intelligence and intellectual rigor, books on book illustration . . . *from Rubens to Daumier*, observes therein that Romeyn de Hooghe was the greatest etcher of the Dutch seventeenth century after Rembrandt. It is, to be sure, an idle, absurd and unprovable assertion, but, through it, we are privy to Benesch's high esteem for the generally unnoticed de Hooghe, who was indubitably Holland's and probably Europe's greatest book illustrator of the seventeenth century. His energy and his production were prodigious, he kept the Kalverstraat and the publishers well-supplied with copper plates. To gauge his greatness, de Hooghe must be seen in works that are unquestionably from his hands; he ran an immense shop with the likes of the talented Schoonboeck Haardwijn, et alia, often masquerading as their master. There are those artists, and de Hooghe was one, who amaze us by their obsessive levels of productivity. It has been computed that Gustave Doré was put to the fiendish task of feeding the professional reproductive wood engravers at the rate of fifteen drawings a day. Fifteen a day, a bit of a drudge, perhaps, but possible as follows: two drawings before breakfast and three after breakfast, four after lunch, three after dinner and three after supper, and for three hundred and sixty five days; one did not sleep much, and one grew intolerably fat from the general bodily inaction except for one's wrist. The earlier protean creators tended to have huge ateliers with many pupils, apprentices, assistants executing the master's intentions: thus Rubens's oil sketches which are from his superlative hands are universally extolled and esteemed, whilst there are constant and interminable squabbles as to the extent of his involvement in a painting's realization. De Hooghe's work must be subjected to that same judgemental stringency, a continuous critical winnowing must accompany any consideration of his genius. Within that vast corpus of his works, there are, as in all artists' work, greater and lesser levels of attainment: there is, in de Hooghe's case, because of his unstinting and demonic energy, a wider stretch between his greatest and poorest works. Romeyn de Hooghe is a great Baroque

De Hooghe. drawing. 1987.

orchestrator of huge spaces, inhabited by hordes of jostling figures as in Bidloo's "Koomst de H. Koenig Willem III . . . den Haag" in which the festivities attendant the king's visit are tumultuously rendered, ending with a stupendous burst of fireworks, etched with pyrotechnical palpability. In the "Schouwburg der Staat Nederlands" a series of plates ensues of great depth and complexity, emblematic and deeply symbolic and mystic, a tenebrosity of brilliant lights and darkest shades engulf the very air. Reminiscent, as the light surges and cascades down and deeply scours, groups of figures deposed as Baroque statuary, of Rembrandt's late etching of the "Crucifixion", in its final states. The great wall map of "Rotterdam", immense in scale, its central overweening view of Rotterdam, as seen from the sea extends to ten or more feet, below which is laid out straat by gracht all of Rotterdam, subsequently bombed away in World War Two, and surrounded by the principal buildings of the town. The audacity and power of the handling and the conception take one's cliché-ridden breath away. We marvel at the bold certainty of de Hooghe's needle as it traverses the huge plates without hesitancy or betraying a scintilla of doubt; indeed, here in the "Rotterdam" and in the somewhat smaller "Haarlem" is Baroque sureness building the structures of splendor and grandeur. His illustrations for La Fontaine's *Fables* are by comparison tiny; they are the first illustrations to La Fontaine and are delicious for the intimate interacting of the figures, for the specificity of ambience, indoor and out, and for the delicate eroticisms which make the book a harbinger of the eighteenth century. There is a quickness of line and vivacity of temper in de Hooghe's etchings for Hoogstraten's emblem book, *Het Voorhof der Zille*, and in the very small plates that grace that sweet book of spooks, Lavater's *De Spectris*, Romeyn de Hooghe had the unusual capacity of organizing the most complex of multi-images into a clear and perceptible order; a Baroque quality and propensity; thus the tangle of religious and political symbols, that bewilder if we do not, or cannot, penetrate to their ephemeral seventeenth-century realities, remarkably enough, interest and even entrance us as artistic artifacts. His puissant skills are brilliantly revealed in the monthly etchings he produced for the political journal *Aesopus in Europa* and in the numerous etchings which are exuberantly wild in comic invention and burlesque wit and which were used on broadsides, taking political positions in re this and that. Our inevitable ignorance of the personages depicted and of the intent of their comportments, limits the degree of our pleasure, understanding and enjoyment, but despite our malfeasant incapacities we do participate in the meanings sufficiently for the prints to render their powerful if now limited meanings. De Hooghe is so wondrously diverse that I must go on and briefly describe several other of his richly laden books. One is called in its French edition *Academie de la Lutte,* and it consists of a long series of etchings instructing the nobleman, the merchant, and one hopes the occasional traveling scholar, how to protect themselves against the attacks of murderers, thieves, muggers, coney-catchers and the like. It is a kind of primordial do-it-yourself ju-jitsu and the attacking and the defending positions are persuasively, cunningly and convincingly observed and rendered; the most outlandishly bizarre posture is not beyond de Hooghe's believable rendering. Another book of de Hooghe's describes the great park at Anguinen, ingeniously topiated and arboreally over-wrought, with long tunnels of love, great walls built of giant, thin hedge, using plants as building material, follies, mazes and other extravagances. The book opens with a very vigorous de Hooghe etching of the busy scene outside the château at which the Dukes d'Arenburg made their home, as the seasons moved them. A folding frontispiece has a multitude of coaches and wagons, persons on horseback and afoot all animating and harassing the plein air before the château. De Hooghe etched a similar but considerably longer plate describing a scene of sheerest bustle and wildest hustle, enacted before His Majesty's summer castle at Loo. Published, for reasons unknown to me, deep in the eighteenth century, the lively plate unfolds to a four-footed panorama of Dutch royal pandemonium and bourgeois and peasant hugger-mugger: delightful; the plates of the summer garden are very much in the manner of Anguinen, but wanting their intense freshness and horticultural phantasy. I have been to some length extolling the virtues, the complex beauty and vaulting genius of Romeyn de Hooghe because his entire oeuvre is locked away in essentially inaccessible books. The etching-bearing broadsides are fugitive and very rare, as are those larger topical prints issued to commemorate specific events, such as the two beautiful prints showing the exterior and interior of the Amsterdamian Spanish

169

and Portuguese synagogue on the occasion of its opening. Otto Benesch is entirely justified in his estimations of de Hooghe; there is no Dutch seventeenth-century etcher or engraver of book illustrations that is his compare. He did not paint, and only forty-one accepted drawings are known; he must have drawn constantly, the drawings being consumed in their transference to the copper-plates. Romeyn de Hooghe is generally unknown, art that glows in books tends to glow unseen; which is a great pity, as witness his series of etchings in the tradition of Jacques Callot and indicative of Goya, Kollwitz and Dix which he made to illustrate Wiquefort's *Adivis Fidèle* which reports in detail the horrors committed by the French in their invasion of Holland. De Hooghe drives his excoriating needle into the unallayed depiction of terror and images describing ghastly disintegrative exacerbation in which cruelty and the horrific are successive as they struggle for prominence in these representations of war's despicable depredation and deprivation. To see the masterworks of Romeyn de Hooghe one must apply to the rare book rooms and print cabinets where the books and prints are housed; their perusal will quicken the dry paper into flaming life.

De Hooghe. we. 1968.

Adam Elsheimer

On 14 January 1611 Peter Paul Rubens wrote to his doctor, friend and sometimes agent, Dr J. Faber, ". . . but the second [letter] . . . was the bearer of the most cruel news – that of the death of our beloved Signor Adam, – which was very bitter to me. Surely, after such a loss, our entire profession ought to clothe itself in mourning. It will not easily succeed in replacing him . . . . He has died in the flower of his studies, and adhuc sua messis in herba erat. [His wheat was still in the blade. Ovid, Heroides, 17, 263.] One could have expected of him res nunquam visae nunquam videndae; in summa ostendenunt terris hunc tantum fata. [Things that one has never seen and never will see; in short, destiny had only shown him to the world. Aeneid 6.869.] For myself, I have never felt my heart more profoundly pierced by grief than at this news, and I shall never regard with a friendly eye, those who have brought him to so miserable an end." Rubens's letter further expresses his hope for the removal to Flanders of one of Elsheimer's paintings on copper and specifically mentions, "Flight of our Lady into Egypt". It is pleasantly and reassuringly odd to see the mighty and flesh-loving Apelles of the North so moved at the death of Elsheimer; the painter of huge and mighty works, vast machines such as the cycle dealing with Catherine de Medici which involved a mass of assistants grinding and priming, under-painting and over-painting, glazing and varnishing, all leading and building to that final Rubensian laying-on of hands, the touch that coheres; it is decidedly singular that the heart of the protean Rubens should so cleave to the departed master of the tiniest panels. They glowed with an uncanny flame and were like sudden minute bolts of brilliancy; and Rubens like all artists who knew them in Elsheimer's time and since have hearkened to their intense inscapédness and their sublimities of form and color. Elsheimer worked the minute surfaces of his copper panels with the smallest imaginable brushes (reminding one of those mythic one- and two-haired brushes that the Venetians accused the Flemings of working with, with further implications of devilish intervention – their disbelief and bewilderment doubtlessly increased and the brushes became more diabolically diminutive when they confronted the paintings of Dürer). It was slow, arduous, knuckle-breaking, fatiguing,

171

flesh-bruising, time-consuming work, entirely suitable to his personality as adduced by Sandrart, who says he was very meditative and accuses him of "endlessly musing in front of nature". There are suggestions of his being depression-prone, but, "il diavolo perghi cose piccoli," and it was said of him: "that he painted on a large scale within a small compass": it is remarkable to see the persevering tiny monumentality, blown, via a slide-projector, into the immense scale of Tintoretto and Veronese without suffering any diminution of grand splendor, and the light-expanded forms are now massive, ponderous and imposing, as indeed they are in their tiny circumscribed spaces. Myths and tales of all sorts abound in the historical record and its peripheral accruement, about so magical a painter as "Signor Adam", as he was universally called: there is doubtless a false tradition that Elsheimer was lazy and slothful, given to long periods of dereliction and inactivity. Another legend has him in deepest poverty, for as Sandrart reports, ". . . his method of working prevented him from completing enough to make a living:" although Baglione asserts that "the Apostolic Palace administered to them [his Scottish wife and numerous children] a reasonable subsistence." Baglione is the contemporary source of this oddment: "He died young of a stomach complaint, it is said, caused by painting so many small pieces with so much effort . . . he died of exhaustion. He was a good-looking man of noble presence." Sandrart, the German Vasari, notes that "Adam Elsheimer not only invariably attempted difficult things, but he was able to accomplish them splendidly." Elsheimer persuasively controls our eyes as they roam over his tiny paintings, he drives our eyes relentlessly through the narrowest side-angled passageways, on into central planes, where action and inaction often proceed together, and farther into the distant recesses of landscape and templed hills and ruin-strewn plains. And there is an uncanny sense of time frozen, an effect similar to a movie projector slowly showing one unrelated unmoving frame after motionless frame. All of the stones in "The Stoning of St Stephen" are about to be thrown, none are mid-air; and within the stalled time, the inaction has contrasting active and passive components. The hugely turbaned Turkish prince, dressed in dazzling silks, and his accompanying page in red velvets are part of a crowd of mute and passive watchers, indifferent and yet somehow

172

Elsheimer. drawing. 1955.

173

apprehensive, regarding the ghastly martyrdom; and the pain-palliating angel stopped in its rushing tumble from heaven, hovers in quivering glory above the scene, yielding a beneficent solace to the already bleeding saint. The stoners form a deadly semi-circle around St Stephen. The scene and its figures are suffused with a heightened, heavenly shaft of light, an Elsheimer light that bathes the participants in revelatory purity and clarity, but not without its deep and sudden darkness, that opens Sheol-like at the knees of the tortured saint. "St Lawrence being prepared for Martyrdom", a somewhat smaller picture of the same date, 1600, is composed of motifs similar to the "St Stephen". What is most arresting in the "St Lawrence" is its anticipatory tension expressed in the saint's impending death; thus the eye is torn away from the white-robed saint, away from the grave figures surrounding and preparing him, toward the preparations of the deadly gridiron where the Lawrencian broiling, the heathen fry-up will proceed. We look with dread at the flaming coals that are being carried in and raked over the fiery bed. But Signor Adam provides us with an escape; our eyes push past the Apollonian Hercules that stonily surveys the scene, past the fire-tenders, past a crush of onlookers, through a pergolated arch, and up into the peaceful hills and a rising, reassuring temple and pagan peace. Above the martyr, a beautiful angel in oppositional parity to the surprisingly handsome Hercules (beautiful youthful messengers of ugly, old gods) invests the scene with a supernal and supernatural beauty and proves a reassuring testament against the impending martyrdom. Along with the passive and the active, there is, in these paintings, an opposition of pagan and Christian, that deepens their meanings, and enriches their intentions. The St Lawrence was once owned by the brilliant painter Paul Bril; apparently Elsheimer and Bril had a deep and fruitful friendship, influencing one the other and enlarging each other's vision. The "Aurora" painted some six years later is a profound exemplar of the quality in Elsheimer which Keith Andrews so acutely termed "elegiac meditation". Time is made to stop in its golden morning flight, the brights swelling over and onto the deep un-sun-touched darks, which approach the day with that same inevitability that wakes humans into the fields and hills. The figures at lower left, deep in the obscurant shadows, preparing for the emergent, the intrusive sun, are thought to be painted by another hand, and Goudt's engraving after the painting cuts away that section of it (Goudt owned the painting, and of Goudt, more anon). Adam Elsheimer had studied with that curious master Philip von Uffenbach, who was a living link to Grünewald and who was meant to own a group of Grünewald drawings, that descended to him from his master who was a student of a son of Grünewald. It delights me that Grünewald reaches from the early sixteenth century to prod Elsheimer in the early seventeenth century; there is a mighty pull in the wave of history. Elsheimer left for Italy in 1599, traveling throughout Bavaria (and doubtlessly seeing many Altdorfers, a crucial source for him: it was Altdorfer's, not Caravaggio's vision that spurred and plenished Elsheimer's conception of painting the night), arriving in Rome in 1599, with ten years left of life and work. Elsheimer was the arch-depicter of the traveling "Tobias and the Angel" theme. It was a subject of emergent interest to the seventeenth-century burghers, who were beginning to send their sons away to school, as Julius Held brilliantly shows in *Rembrandt and the Book of Tobit*: the theme became the expressive device to insure safe passage, a kind of ex-voto in advance. The heartening lack of sentimentality in these touching scenes of Tobias, protected by the disguised angel, Raphael, carrying and lugging and dragging the great curative fish, is refreshing. Seghers based an etching on Elsheimer's "Large Tobias", the copper of which Rembrandt owned and which he altered to a "Flight into Egypt", leaving the landscape essentials unchanged. Elsheimer's depictions were replicated many times in prints by himself, Goudt and others, and became the theme's main source. The heart-warming pagan story of "Jupiter and Mercury in the House of Philomon and Baucis" is strikingly reminiscent of the angelic visitation to Abraham and Sarah. The painting is powerfully and dramatically lit from below, prophetic of the Rembrandt who painted the Jacquemart-André "Supper at Emmaus". A double disguise occurs in the rude hut: the gods traveling as poor, homeless, and helpless beggars, and the sweet nobility of the ancient couple which is disguised by their stance of peasant-ignorant humility. Their selfless generosity is rewarded by Jupiter who, at their deaths, transforms them into great oak trees, entwined in a loving embrace through eternity, a fitting end and an apt Ovidian metamorphosis. I will

Elsheimer. drawing. 1960.

forswear a description of its lambency, for I cannot forestall an imminent consideration of my all-time favorite Elsheimer, his "Flight into Egypt". Painted in 1609, it is a spectacle of light piercing, with the force of primal creation, the deep density of night. Elsheimer's name was to be associated with night pieces through the ages, and it was little wonder that Rubens wanted "The Rest on the Flight into Egypt" to be removed and vested in Flanders. The source of light in this amazing painting is tri-fold: the new-risen moon reflected to a greater silvery glow in the pond, its sudden flourish of brightness contained by the darkened trees at the pond's edge, seem to consume the light; the flickering flambeau in the hand of Joseph, picking out in quavering delicacy the lineaments of Mary, the Christ child and himself; and the hot fire of the shepherds which sends a trail of sparks flying upwards to join the great empyrean, in its deepest, richest, nocturnal glory; the milky way, the sky's diadem in full incandescent flow, the planets and the stars spread in blazing wonder against the blackened sky. How the light-maddened Rembrandt must have relished that picture or Goudt's incredibly fine print of it. Hendrick Goudt, Palatinate count, his life and work is knotted with Elsheimer's. Legends and myths abound, alternately binding them together in unbreakable friendship and dependency, or torn apart, acting, behaving like enemies; can one believe that Goudt had Elsheimer thrown into debtor's prison or that he was responsible for his release? What is true beyond the understanding is the miracle of Goudt's masterful copper-engraving, exemplified in the seven plates he engraved after Elsheimer's paintings. The miracle is in the supreme quality of each engraving. Can one imagine anyone engraving only seven plates, each proving to be a masterwork of graphic art? One can detect no development in sureness of handling, no evidence of maturation in technique, no slow-sure advance from print to print until mastery is achieved: no, it is as though Goudt proceeded to total engraving skills through the frontal lobes of Jove. The subtle tonalities of light crepuscular and candled light, caught and reflected, traced and refracted in enlarged and diminished luminescence from spacious space to cramped space, are all rendered in the refractory metal with breath-taking skill. Those seven engravings assault my sensibilities, they astound me for the mystery of their making and for their relentless beauty. Goudt is so emburrowed into Elsheimer's marrow that he becomes a species of Elsheimer. Their drawing styles are virtually indistinguishable and Elsheimer's corpus of accepted drawings has drastically dwindled. The effect is of a doppelgänger, of Goudt's entirely assuming, like the putting on of a greatcoat, the personality, quality and characteristics of Adam Elsheimer's art, indeed, adapting the very habitude of Elsheimer. Andrews says of him, ''Goudt lacked an original mind and had to feed on the imagination of others . . . . But even if Goudt was unimaginative, he had undoubted skill, as even his most undisciplined scribble demonstrates. Like a parasite he fed on his 'host'. He became mentally deranged later in life and one wonders whether signs of instability . . . may have accounted for his ambivalent behaviour towards Elsheimer.'' Those seven engravings were broadcast across Europe and the small paintings and tiny oeuvre of Elsheimer had a vast impact. Andrews speaks of deeper levels in Elsheimer's art affecting Rembrandt and Claude. Those deeply contemplative paintings had played a generative rôle in the evolvement of seventeenth-century painting. Elsheimer's paintings haunt the imaginative memory; like night-glowing jewels, the immensity of these works seep into the serried crevices of our minds and lodge there forever, enlarging our vision and deepening our understanding.

Elsheimer. drawing. 1987.

Caspar David Friedrich

Heinrich Heine explosively defined Romanticism as "a red rose sprung from the blood of Christ", and how aptly that searing phrase characterizes the turbulence of Delacroix and Géricault; but what of the atmospheric phantasies of Turner or the carnal obsessions of Etty, or the stilled, the haunted marshes of Heade, or the intense lush bitter-sweetness of Romako, or the moon-maddened visions of Palmer, or the deep, hushed sonorities of Caspar David Friedrich? Indeed, one cannot treat of Romanticism, one must consider Romanticisms. That allows us to couple as Romantics such diversities as Carrière, whose sfumato-misted visions of Maternité are unique, and Rethel, who convincingly dances death, the hierarchical stations in a medieval-like ambience, and Böcklin, whose dream-like but sentimental invention "The Isle of Death" proved a pervasive and influential symbol, and Ryder, whose moon-encrusted ships sail uncharted seas, and Friedrichian landscapes stretched long in beaten silver and driven greens. Romanticism compacts unto itself the Burkean horrific exemplified in Fuseli, the Rosaesque banditry which inspired Mortimer, the urban poor pressing in Daumier's bounteous and beautiful designs against prevalent inequities and injustices, the vivid liveliness that van Mares infused into neo-Classical modes, the crushed jewelry of color in Monticelli's flower pieces and fêtes galantes and champêtres, and the very still, air-filled landscapes of Caspar David Friedrich. Indeed, it does make some sense to speak of a work as Romantic; we assuredly aver that the work is free of Poussinesque order with the "Ideal" achieved, and not a work of Expressionistic tumult, that surge toward the extremities of the modalities of expressive picture-making. Thus the term Romanticism is a useful negative, informing us at the least of a tendency and, at the best, fixing the boundaries of the artist's endeavor between Classicism and Expressionism. "Friedrich is the landscapist of a totally Nordic, Ossian-like nature, abundant of icy air, and the Baltic Sea cliffs which are lapped by its dark waters" (R. von Lilienstern in 1809). Friedrich's panthesizing zeal reels from his landscapes as apparent as a programmatic theological tract. But with infusions of subtlest nuance, with hovering penumbras, are these landscapes endowed and

179

Friedrich. drawing. 1986.

180

bestrewed and salient with the silences trapped within stiffnesses. Did Bergman learn the opening of his "Fifth Seal" from Friedrich's "Monk Walking Along the Sea"? But how vast is Freidrich's sky, how laden with foreboding, how finite and tiny the small but essential figure; and those blue valleys and bluer glaciers that stretch our eyes into infinity. His entirely silent landscapes are often outfitted with ruins, a Romantic preoccupation, indeed, a Romantic invention; but always ruins of monasteries and abbeys or churches, and even the ruins of trees, huddled together in desolate devotion, shivering in a kind of ecclesiastical closeness and fervor. The very air of his broad-viewed landscapes seems to breathe of that spiritual essence, that Romantic renunciation of the actual for the ideal, for the mystic coupling of heaven and earth, all aglow in transcendental harmony, in the incandescent after-image, vibrating at the uniting of the mundane and the celestial. But Caspar David Friedrich's most beautiful and most moving paintings more directly concern human beings, very often those shore-bound persons, usually wives or mothers or sweethearts gazing out to sea, with "the seal's wide spindrift gaze toward paradise" for the sight of a reappearing sail or the last, heart-clenching moments of a disappearing top-mast. Inevitably these figures sit alone or in groups, with their backs toward us seen in very dark silhouette against the glowing, last sun-drenched sea. These paintings are charged with the sharpest melancholia, haunted with the chronic sadness of those who sail the seas and the unassuageable anxiety of those who await their return. The sea is always gentle in these paintings, the instilled feeling is always heightened, verging on the beatific; these works become in the end a kind of religious offering, an affirmation of hope, a beneficent ex-voto, the sustainer over the long months of restless, painful waiting. Friedrich's landscapes are all aglow with a deep sense of peace, whether of dazzling alpine views, or uprearing hillocks at dawn, whether sighting down a treacherous, dizzying declivity cut into the cliffs, and pell-mell tearing one's gaze to the sea, or the solitary confrontational presence of a great, aged, scruffy tree, laden with unyielding snow. In that near-spectral still silence that is so characteristic of Friedrich's landscapes, the very air seems thinned, clarified, charged with the purity of deeper and longer apprehension, a greater lucidity, a wider perception, a more intense seeing. In the "Wreck of the Hope" the great crags and mighty splinters of ice are perceived in a geometric cold crystalline clearness. One must search for the Hope crushed in the remorseless, upthrusting, crashing magnitudes of ice. No figures can be seen; no survivors are scurrying about, they are unnecessary, the picture is about the mighty primacy of nature. In Sturm und Drang, human beings tend to be reduced to near invisibility as Nature's vastness dominates, indeed, overwhelms. Gogol teaches this in a trenchant story: a wanderer is lost, and wanders through endless caverns, plunging ever downwards, deeper and deeper, until he is in a huge cave, so immense that he realizes that he has inadvertently blundered into the very center of earth. At the center of the center sits a colossus, larger beyond measure than his conception could conjure up or imagine; he understood that he was in the presence of God. God was brooding. He was immobile, sitting trance-like, in deepest thought. The wanderer approached the awesome figure, and said, "Tell me, oh God, what aspect of human necessity are you pondering?" "I am considering," answered God, "whether to strengthen the muscle on the rear leg of the flea." It is the tenet taught by Ossian, the supposed primal bardic epochal epic-making that swept Europe at the end of the eighteenth century. Caspar David Friedrich was born at Greifswald, the site of those lonely harbor-side idylls, in 1774, and received academic training from Johann Gottfried Quistorp. In 1794, aged twenty, he traveled to Copenhagen and entered the Academy of Art, the center of painterly instruction and of culture generally for the towns bordering on the Baltic Sea. The paradigm for Friedrich was the proto-Romantic Asmus Jacob Carstens, who had attended the Copenhagen academy, and Friedrich was followed there by the mysterious and tragic Philip Otto Runge. The school was free and all gifted Scandinavians attended it. Friedrich was a student of Abilgaard, surely Denmark's greatest painter, the master of a strange, heightened, smooth-surfaced world in which drugged figures seem frozen in stance, gesture, and action. Abilgaard had been strongly influenced by Fuseli; they moved in the same circles in Rome. Friedrich had observed, in 1830, a somewhat anti-school feeling: "Not having been instructed is often a boon for intellectually gifted persons. All the teaching and instructing . . . too easily kills the spiritual . . .

Friedrich. drawing. 1986.

and rouses something like wretchedness to mediocrity." I have noted the crucial rôle of those seaward-gazing figures, but we engage the impersonal backs of the watchers and waiters in those paintings. Occasionally we are confronted by a human face and the inevitable ensuing human psychology. But in his purer landscapes, humans are either absent or reduced to a minimal function. But Friedrich's paintings, for all the Sturm und Drang reductiveness of the human presence, and of the sublimating pantheism of his brand of Romanticism, enlarge our human capacity, our human conceptions of space, our understanding of human endeavor. Thus the ruins of Gothic churches, eerie in moonlight or all mournful in deep snow, however bereft of human beings, are paintings delineating the tracery of human history. The mighty trees are anthropomorphically animated to human sympathy and hearken to human passions. The odd duality of enhancement and reduction of human presence and engagement in these paintings lends them heightened qualities of intensity and diversity, a dialectical dynamic that lifts them to an astonishing power and beauty.

Adolph von Menzel

Adolph von Menzel had the physique of a large dwarf. This tiny
painterly titan was much decorated by the Kaiser, the academies,
principalities, institutes, etc.: one of his particular Prussian orders had
as a perquisite the snapping to instant attention of the famous
Prussian honor guard whenever he appeared. These Prussian
guardians were conscripted from amongst the tallest available men in
Germany, further extended by their Hessian-like upwards-pointed
helmets. There is an inimitable photograph showing the impish
Menzel, determinedly walking through a gauntlet of stiffly attentive,
honor-rendering Prussian guards. The photograph is bizarre, it
contracts and diminishes Menzel and stretches the guards. But that is
the only diminution of Menzel that I know of. Menzel was one of
those rare geniuses who, like Mozart, create as readily and easily as
others breathe; or who give that impression of offhand divine
felicitousness. His drawings are suffused with that uncommon quality
of élan, of effortless ease and grace, and breathe a near spontaneous
effortlessness. This long-lived artist drew constantly, continuously and
endlessly, and a horde of his drawings is treasure for our feasting, for
the enriching of our sensibilities, for the enlarging of our
understanding, for the gratification of our eyes' ravaging, for their
sheer miraculous display of drawing wizardry. Menzel's drawings
explore everything: beyond the numerous views of town and country
scapes, and studies of plants, trees, animals, etc., a great many study
the human "phiz" from every vantage, of men young and old, of
women turned away from one, repeated studies of the outlines of
cheeks, the edges of ears, the backs and sides of necks, and the open-
mouthed look of young girls and long-tressed young women, and
human beings gesturing in every seeming inexhaustible way. Menzel's
is a prodigal outpouring of drawings. Menzel had a near-unique
capacity to picture-forth almost anything, and amazingly he does so
with verve, power and utter conviction. He could draw onto toned
paper with colored chalks, for instance, an eighteenth-century soldier
with tricorn seen from behind, removing his great-coat. The virtuosic
skills necessary to convincingly render such an action, which is simple
in nature but incredibly complex in the delineation, are of the highest

185

order. Menzel illustrated Kugler's monumental life of Frederick the Great with all the expected Menzellian panache and the anticipated snap and sparkle, and with the looked-for inevitable swagger. And how appropriate to the theme: Der Alte Fritz, his campaigns, the frenchified delights of Sans Souci, Voltaire amongst them, the spreading Rococo and the generals and their ladies all spring to the quick in Menzel's vivid, vivacious and brilliant pen drawings breathtakingly translated into wood-engravings by the unbelievable skills of Engelmann and Vogel. Many editions of the Kugler's Frederick were issued with Menzel's illustrations intact; there were expensive, leather-bound many-volumed sets, less expensive one- or two-volume editions, and luxurious ausgaben with the wood-engravings superbly printed on chine appliqué, and the images shone brightly in even the cheapest schoolboy editions. Germans grew up on these illustrations, they conceived of Frederick and his entourage according to Menzel's trenchant tutelage. Menzel, with characteristic ingenious brilliance, executed a remarkable series of lithographs under the general title "Mit Pinzel und Schabeizen"; the subjects range from the "Berne Bear Pit" to an admirable portrait of Molière, in elegant thoughtful mien, pen in hand, wig abundant, his body arched; the predominant ironic poet seems to sizzle in the tight grains printed from the Bavarian limestone. The set is a commendable penetration into the proverbial subtleties of the lithographic zones, discovering with a Menzel-like inevitability the limits of that moment's expressive possibility: "With Brush and Scraper" indeed. It is strange how generally ignorant otherwise knowledgeable people are about nineteenth-century German painting. Persons who without straining could readily name ten to fifteen French painters of that long painting century cannot name a single German artist of those hundred years. The subtlest might pronounce the name of that magical artist Caspar David Friedrich. But their sensibilities have not been assailed and delighted by the works of Adolph von Menzel and other extraordinary painters. How did the French usurp unto themselves all general cognizance of nineteenth-century painting? It is as though painting did not fall forward or backward anywhere else in that smutched and smelly century. It is a further oddment that the century of the industrial revolution, fully geared, the century that instituted the

186

Menzel. etching. 1967.

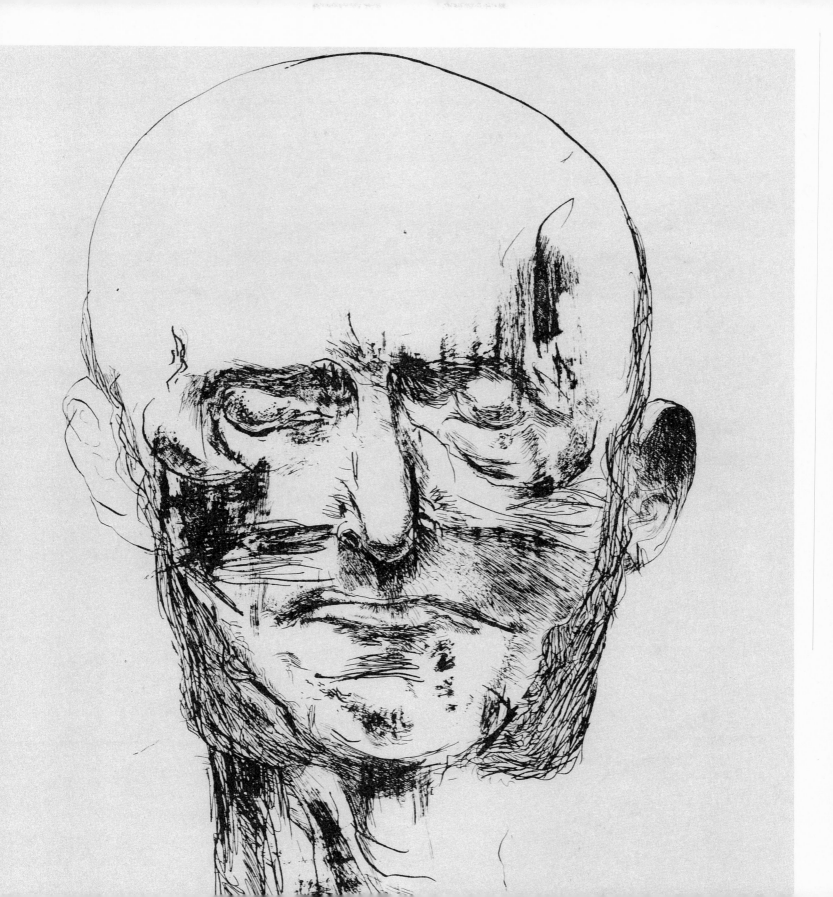

satanic mills, produced as far as I know only three significant depictions of scenes of concerted industrial toil, of scenes of many-handed strain, of scenes of exhausting work within the high-ceilinged, long-sided spaces of the demonic mills, and the best by far is Menzel's. And he painted his studio, a newly romanticized workspace, perhaps replacing the alchemist's study; if the newer impedimenta did not quite equal the suspended giant lizards, the glowing crucibles, and the glistening beakers and retorts, for heightened dazzle, they in their later development, with Turkish corners and the quasi-Near Eastern paraphernalia strewn artfully about, make for an admirable successor. Menzel painted his studio wall, lit from below, the wall hung with many a curiosity amongst which hangs the death-mask of Canova in great advanced age, the lower jaw slung far forward in extreme prognathic agedness; and a fresh painting of his sister in a new gown, and family scenes seen by day and at night. Menzel painted the panoply of royalty and its inevitable and aberrant nobility, all painted with dash and spirit. Menzel was a superb painter with a compelling understanding of the physical fabric and the plasticity of picture making.

Lovis Corinth

God's creating Adam in his own likeness looms large in the annals of narcissism, but painters rendering themselves in self-portraits form a phalanx directly behind God. But a veritable flood of narcissism flowed from those artists that were life-long obsessed with the depiction of themselves. The visual self-revelations, the time-lapse autobiographical friezes, the continual public self-examination are characteristic of but a few artists, but they are masters of the greatest primal power. Rembrandt surveyed his countenance unendingly; grimacing, peering, surveying, prying, probing, scanning, conning or staring, his face serenely or severely composed, the visage implacable, deeply and mysteriously human in its monumental stiffness. Munch was another searcher in the telling mirrors, and we can traverse his time from age to age until he is frozen into the layered anxieties of old age, clad in pajamas, standing stiffly at his bedside. The paintings, drawings and prints reveal aspects of Munch's perception of reality, dazed in the extremes of Expressionistic angst or lapsed into the melancholia of a blue-green bar-room. The pursuit of his visage unrelenting, not even daunted by the actuality of death in the frontal plane; not the fake fiddle-playing death of Böcklin, but the palpable deadly reality of death, its presence thickening the atmosphere into contained, soundless, open-mouthed hysteria; its presence staining the canvas into stiffening stillness. Käthe Kollwitz, the supreme political artificer, reveals the torments of her age in the lineaments of her face as it proceeds from virtual schoolgirl through all the ages of womanhood, till the great black hulking image of herself in old age, a bulwark bastioned against the Nazi depredation and filth. Her "Ewige Antlitz" mirrors the years of violent change, the undertows of uprisings, wars, revolts, oppression and the personal tragedy of a beloved son lost in the horrific stupidity of World War One, and the years of observing and solicitude for the poverty-smitten of Berlin. That grief-stricken but ever-resolute face and head confront our awestruck gaze from woodcut and etching, drawing and lithograph. Lovis Corinth, a near contemporary of Käthe Kollwitz, was a prodigious painter whose painted oeuvre is vast and extraordinary for the range and variety of paintings painted and objects depicted:

Corinth. monotype. 1980.

Corinth is precariously poised between the liberated academicism of Liebermann and the onrushing Expressionism of Kirchner. He developed a bold, slashing, post-Slevogtian style of great strength, bravura, swagger, and complexity. And Lovis Corinth loved to paint himself, indeed, he was a protean maker of self-portraits, a passion that proved constant throughout his life: his self-portraits disclose him to us and as frequently hide him from our penetrating gaze. One perceives in the innumerable images his physical progression through life. We behold Corinth sighing and grieving, dour and scowling, frowning, whistling, sneering; he is passive, he is active, he presents himself to us in every human guise. In 1925 he dons in a colored pencil drawing the crown of thorns, and like Dürer, becomes the Salvator Mundi. He is the world-engulfing youngster, the thickened artist in early middle years and suddenly grown old and paralyzed, palsied with Parkinsonism perhaps, and how aptly he turned his handicap to the stylistic niceties of Expressionism. He slashes at the canvas, the dabs accommodating his ''intention tremor'' become an extension of his natural manner. He painted himself in paralysis, still buoyantly strong, upright in posture, catching and reflecting his fading nimbus, the departing, golden god-head. His phantasies are audacious in their variety; now he is a helm-bearing knight, recklessly careening about, and then a neck-tied doctor dangling a skeleton, but its meaning is not medical, it is a ''vanitas'', a ''memento mori''. Corinth stuns us as he slips from rôle to unexpected rôle. Open and closed, Corinth's self-portraits frame a dynamic dialectic in which phantasy and reality are mingled; the one reinforcing the other, allowing the wildest imaginings the appearance of reality, the lineaments of actuality. In a painting Corinth turns himself into a fat, still virile, aged Silenus, cavorting and tumbling with buxom, naked nymphs. He paints himself into these scenic events with bravado, with reckless intensity, with the blandishment of bright and strong contrasting color. At the Fine Arts Museum, Montreal, Corinth wears a fur cap; he is the intrepid hunter; elsewhere he wears the large-brimmed, slouched felt hat of Bohemia: the guises are near endless. In a long series of etchings and lithographs Corinth examines himself from close up. The fair young likeness grows from one print's time to another till he emerges, with total probity, into haggard, palsied old age.

191

Ernst Barlach

A funereal photograph shows the dead Barlach tucked into a tufted
samite-sheathed coffin looking like a baby snug in a bassinet: the
mightiest of Germans appears weak and infantile in the dishonest
sentimentalish photograph. The photograph betrays in the shrunken
and reduced corpse of Barlach a sense of the obloquy heaped on him
by the Nazis. The photograph yields not a hint of Barlach's strength
and fearlessness, nor of his intransigence, nor of his glorious
obdurance and obstinance. Although harassed and brutalized he was
steadfast in his public and announced hatred of the fascists and it was
a sad blessing that death saved him from the depths of the depraved
depredation that the Nazi filth would have put him to: instead they
tore down and destroyed his five public monuments. Brecht observed
in his notes to a Barlach Exhibition, "It is said, that Barlach made his
'Laughing Old Woman' when he heard that many of his sculptures,
removed from the museums as decadent, were being sold in
Switzerland to hook foreign money for the manufacturing of
cannons." Ernst Barlach died on 24 October 1938. Like many artists
before and since him, he found his time bereft of a naturally
monumental style that his concepts demanded. Monumentality in
sculpture is the issue of communal participation in the meaning of the
sculpture: monumental sculpture in the past was crucially engaged
with myth and religion: let myth here be understood as in Ernest
Cassiere's concept that myth expresses an ideal of a society and
religion in its generally understood meaning as a communality of
participation and belief; thus the Egyptian pharaoh was perceived as a
god by everyone in ancient Egypt and with what resulting massive
monumentality in expressing the universality of that godliness: thus
too the Greek myths worked a vision of monumentality in ancient
Greece; early Christianity was a belief that inspired and animated the
whole society, and the cathedrals and the sculpture of the
Romanesque and early Gothic are an expression of that shared
wholeness, a sodality of participation. The artists in times of
monumentality tend to be anonymous. When these conditions change,
when myth moves into private ways as it did in the early Renaissance,
a system of myths develops that concerns only one class; the myths

192

Barlach: dead, poplar. 1959.

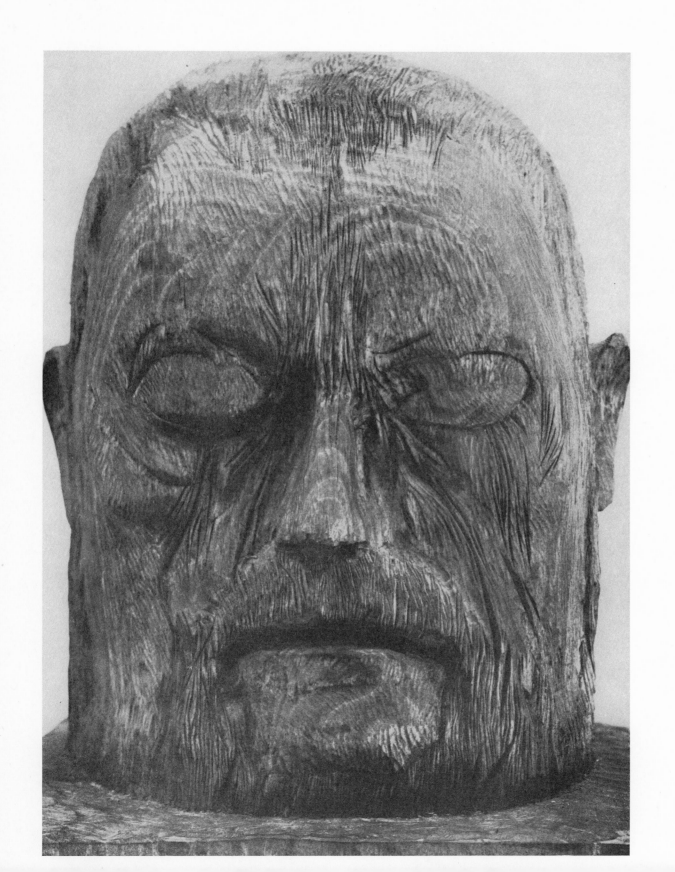

are decidedly exclusive, for instance, the myths of courtly honor, of chastity, of love, etc., and the artist as personality, and as a genius emerges. This happened in third-century Greece, in Rome and in Europe after the thirteenth century. Barlach thus cast about in past art, seeking the praxis, the formal configurations, the plastic strength to contain his timeless content. So too had Blake to invent a mythology in which to load his monumental poetics: so too Henry Moore to Aztec sculptures, so too Yeats finding hermetic monumentality in Celtic myths. Naturally Barlach turned to his heritage and found succor and manner in the Romanesque and early Gothic wood carving of Germany; he found disposed in these deft complexities of form, portions of a language that was essential to his needs, to the monumental forms of Western Europe he added the large modalities of Egyptian sculpture; those subtle envelopes of stone provided the structured armature on which Barlach fused and molded the Gothic devices: what ensued was the unique voice we instantly recognize as Ernst Barlach. Barlach was consumed in his sculpture with the struggle to express and to communicate abstract human states: loneliness, joyousness, abjection and dejection, revenge, fear, old age, pain: as he said: "Just as my mother tongue is the only one that suits me best, so my artistic language is the human figure or the object which or in which humans live, suffer, rejoice, feel, think. I cannot overcome this. Indeed only the elemental emotions of the human race are great and eternal. The things that arrest my attention are what a human being has suffered and is able to endure, his and her greatness including myth and dreams of the future." Although Barlach was thematically committed to generalizing abstract states, his sculpture moves us because he makes the universal to be perceived through the means of a single figure; "The Lonely One" stands for all loneliness, "The Avenger" avenges in communal ferocity, "The Stargazer" contemplates a shared questing for meaning. Barlach so contumaciously confronts these generalities that we experience our own histories in perceiving the sculpture, and we are driven by those wonderful carvings and bronzes into the heat of emotion revealed. The sculptures gleam with the veritable justness of the emotion displayed, they are radiant with apt honesty, lustrous in their driving relentlessly to the inmost heart of truth. The possibility of remoteness

194

Barlach. etching [detail]. 1962.

Barlach. we. 1957.

and distance engendered by these sculptures of abstract states is further minimized by Barlach's happy tendency to employ the ordinary, the usual, the common to probe towards the broadest communion of reality and meaning; Barlach, in this, is the arch anti-Romantic, no Sturm-und-Drang-exhorting of his single-minded conceptualizing figures to dramatic posturing, no Wagnerian Rhine-stinking hocus-pocus, no Georgish chivalrics, and no Kandinsky-like decoration; just the shivering old woman and the meandering old man, the cripple and the singer, the wind-blown and the weary; the quality of humanity so acutely and accurately realized to speak to our emotional understanding and to make each figure personify that condition and that reality. His massive bronze angel, a memorial at Gustrow Cathedral suspended and afloat like a gigantic swollen silence descending into one's consciousness, its vast presence hovers in the stillness of memory and memorializing. Barlach's memorial at Kiel University is an odd work: an angel stands two-square on the arching back of a panther or cougar or fierce wolf and/or lion; the angel holds a large sword and one wonders at the work's purport; the work is strongly steeped in an alien mysticism, a note only very rarely heard in Barlach. Is the angel redemptive? expiative? a revenging angel? purgative? restrictive? in the manner of the sword-revolving protector at the Pearly Gates, or simply an image of non-specified dread, the arching great cat, intense and frightening, the tense sword-wielding angel, imploring Nie Wieder Krieg. Whatever its exact meaning it sits in the memory like a great leaden weight. Early in the century Barlach went to Russia; I do not know the impulsion for the trip, but the effect was deep, especially his visit to the Russian steppes, the great empty grasslands verging towards the endless tundra. He later carved a "Steppenfrau", filling the large-framed body with forms that are redolent of that treeless and wild place; he modeled at least two "Russische Bettlers" and late in his life he carved an old woman chthonian in her earth-clinging Russianness, and one has a sense that those figures pulling greatcoats tighter unto themselves are further expressions of that trip. There is a photograph showing Maillol and Barlach standing on the steps of a museum somewhere in Europe; in the photograph Maillol stands on a step below Barlach yet towers above him; there is an Olympian suavity in the long and languid Frenchman, while Barlach is short, intense, crabbéd with a Gothic visage; the photograph inevitably reveals in the physiognomic stances the two sculptors' great differences, the long silken beard against the stubby coarse one. Maillol is holding, I think, a felt hat while Barlach wears a flat cap. Soon after his return from study in France and from his steppenreise, Barlach published a drawing manual; emphasizing decorative figure work, it is in the long tradition of model-books, manuals of instruction which begin in the Middle Ages. Barlach's book is strongly flavored by Art Nouveau and it is bizarre to see adumbrated here in sinuously flowing lines what will appear later in a powerful Expressionistic mode. The Russian Beggar is in the book, as are designs for chimney pieces, other architectural sculpture designs and many other familiar Barlachian motifs. Barlach was a versatile genius, the author of many plays, in a somewhat oddly archaic German, splendid enough for one of his plays to achieve the Kleist prize. He was a draughtsman of subtle strengths exploring many themes, searching with form-building lines the lineaments of his sculptures. Barlach was a graphic artist of great inventiveness, skill and finesse; he was particularly a master of the woodcut. The incomparable Käthe Kollwitz despaired in her day-books of ever achieving the heights of Barlach in his prints. She extolled his profound humanity. The inevitabilities in his means and in his ends. A series such as ''Die Wandeln Gottes'' discloses Barlach's varied graphic skills and gifts. The series is gloriously free of all clichés, it is a quintessentially Barlachian vision of the Almighty disporting in various guises; hovering in one print in a very God-like attitude, overlooking all of His works; exposing in another instance His great and mightly procreative stomach. Barlach calls this print ''Gottesbauch'' or again in the last woodcut of the set God rests aristocratically among the rocks, looking like a superattenuated Maximilian, Emperor of the Holy Roman Empire. Barlach cut a set of woodcuts, became famous for Goethe's ''Walpurgisnacht'', delighting in the Sabbath, the witches' wild cavorting, their deviltries and their spellbinding. Was it the vigor of his intellect, the steadfastness of his commitment, the degree of his interest, the reach of his genius that allowed Barlach to escape the rancid sentimentality that oft mars the achievement of his German colleagues, and that inherent tendency in Expressionism to virtually

Barlach. we. 1957.

Barlach. we. 1957.

197

simultaneously produce works of the greatest excellence and works of equally great indifference? Ernst Barlach forged within the framework of Expressionism a constant and unique stylistic language, always under his control in both sculpture and prints, which granted him passage to the deeper ranges of human aspiration, longing, despair, joy, and hope.

Barlach. monotype. 1979.

Paula Modersohn Becker

Paula M. Becker is one of those generative artists whose driving
passion and daring innovativeness set her beside Munch as the
progenitors of Expressionism. Her work stretches from the peasant-
touched, jugendstil-tinged symbolism of Heinrich Vogler, through the
freer but still hesitant, cautious, passive, covert, even witless
Barbizonisms of Worpswede, to the striking and strident Expressionist
embrace of form and color. That embrace was a squeeze of ardency,
was an infusing clutch of pictorial strength and of endlessly enlarged
possibility. It was a clasping onto the fire, the coupling with ferocity,
wildness, immediacy, the opting for the flood and its onrushing
energies. Expressionism, fully developed, achieves a miraculous
loosing of control over the act of picture making, with near
incalculable impact on the post-war art of our time. Paula M. Becker
died at an intolerably young age. There is a sentimental tale that heaps
greater pathos on her young death. At a party celebrating the birth of
her daughter, ten days earlier, when the baby was placed in Paula M.
Becker's arms, she is purported to have said, "Schade" (shame), and
died. Paula Becker had said, in 1900, "I know I shall not live very
long. But why is that so sad? Is a festival more beautiful because it
lasts longer? My sensuous perceptions grow sharper, as if I were
supposed to take in everything within the few years that will be
offered to me . . . ." That premature dying robbed her time and ours
of her pulsing power, of her furled glorious color, of her exploration of
new themes. In her brief tenure as a painter, a mere ten years, her
work is constantly splendid, as it develops, evolves and changes. One
inevitably picks and chooses the work that suits one's sensibilities
best: thus my favorite works of hers fall into two different and distinct
periods. I love those paintings, heavy in texture and brilliant in color,
that make monuments out of old peasant women. They sit in their
depths of woolens; chthonian, as though they have been sitting
through time, which, of course, I must remind myself, they have. And
I love Paula M. Becker's self-portraits, nearly all of them, mysterious
and secretive, midst strange immense fronds and leaves; and her
unique self-portraits in pregnancy. Surely as Robin Weinberg has
pointed out, her portrayals of herself pregnant and her depictions of

mothers and children were original with her. The earlier peasant paintings show the peasant women as though moonstruck and in wide-eyed amazement at the gleaming densities of flowers that have risen up all around them, pushed up by a force chimerical. These are heavy North Germans, Hanseatics, seemingly immobile except for the fluent rivulets of glowing color that flow on, in and about them. It is an agreeably salutary instance of a painter's resorting to necessary inventing or distortion to depict with wondrous conviction the actual, the real. The surfaces of these paintings are heavy with deliberate impasto, at its thickest resembling low-relief. Paula M. Becker abandons that heavy texturing in her later painting, although the painting surfaces never suggest anything but the vigorous application of oil and pigment and medium to canvas. There are no other paintings like those peasant women and children of Paula Becker's; they strike with that familiar thump of immediacy that hits us when we confront a van Gogh portrait, and with that dazzling vibrancy that lifts from the surfaces of Montecelli still-lives, and that feeling of silvered inevitability that enshroud the figures in Corot's non-landscape paintings. She is a framer of masterworks that bespeak her uniqueness; a self-portrait drawing of 1898/9 draws one into its seething essences. The young artist, the burgeoning master of a new manner, looks out with an impassioned intensity; there is an odd mixture of angst and expectancy about the gaze, direct yet inquisitive, questioning yet affirming, desiring yet negating: it is a work out of the greatest depths of human sensibility, suffused with a wonderfully enriching ambiguity. It is the sort of drawing which once vested in one's consciousness will not be readily erased. It looms in striking palpability at the peripheries of my artistic fields, where crucial and formative images play. A painting preserved at Bremen called "Woman with a Poppy", dated 1900, seems an ur-Expressionist object of great power and beauty. This painting is prophetic of much that has occurred where attempts have been made to paint the figures with passion, with intensity, and with ecstatic modalities. The "Woman with a Poppy" was wrung from the young artist in a fevered, an exacerbated, an excited passion. There is an immense drawing of circa 1905, of three discrete children, each of natural size, the size of life, and each is absorbed in itself, excluding the two others; and so

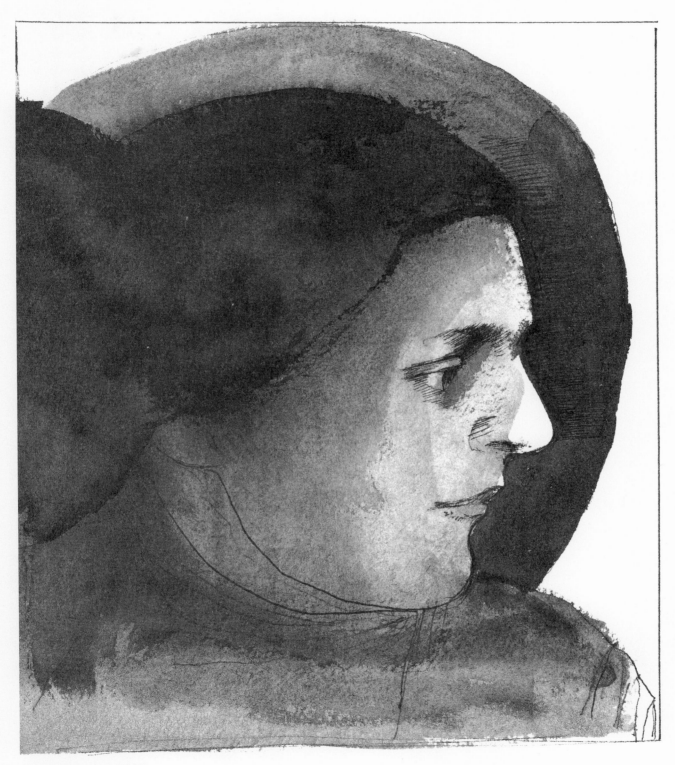

Becker. drawing. 1987.

ominously pervasive is that self-absorption that each child seems to absorb the very fibers of paper on which their images are so magically fixed, entailing unto themselves, so to say, a portion of the drawing. It is of breathtaking fluency and of unallayable impact. I live with that drawing and can attest to the continuity of its smashing impact upon one's being. There is no escaping from it, its great size and its greater artistry assail one's sensibilities, demanding attention and getting it. The three naked separate children are all encased in a deep and brooding melancholia. The children are very thin, but Paula M. Becker did not intend to imply undernourishment; that influence on our perception is the heritage of our miserable century of wars, deprivations, genocides and holocausts. No, they are three profoundly contemplative children, who have been eternally trapped by the grains of her charcoal driven into the surface of the paper. It is a great and beautiful and unforgettable work of art. Paula M. Becker made in her relatively short span, a memorable series of self-portraits. I would speculate that there is an Expressionist element in the making of a long series of self-portraits. There is a self-revelatory tendency that does not connect with Classic or neo-Classic habit. Poussin makes no life-long series of self-portraits, but Rembrandt does; and of the two, Rembrandt surely tends toward Expressionism. I will not be tedious and count the artists who were so possessed by their countenances to repeatedly paint them. I will only point to the great exception to my rule that the neo-Classicist abjured the making of numerous self-portraits; Maurice Quentin de la Tour, an artist/philosopher of the French eighteenth century, who made a series of pastel drawings so evocative of his age, so quizzical, so shy, so wise and all-knowing, so deliberately cynical, that they exist in unique splendor, unlike in affective attitude any other works of the eighteenth century: they also slyly smile, and unforgettably so. Paula M. Becker's self-portraits, on the whole, do not smile at one, yet one's memory sees quizzical half-smiling expressions in several paintings. Paula M. Becker's self-portraits, as one would expect in an artist of her probity, are directly and succinctly revealing. Paintings, luckily, are not read like declaratory sentences, their levels of meaning are not had with simple-minded ease, or with childish clarity, or with polymathic inevitability; and there are no linguistic or any other equivalents. One painting can traverse the surfaces of many moods, or it can be overwhelmingly an expression of a single emotion. Paula M. Becker's self-portraits, nude and pregnant, are entirely without compare before her. This extraordinary and innovative artist paints herself in the mingled tonalities of joy and anguish. She was ambitious, ferociously serious, hampered and harassed by family and by social attitudes; she was powerful, genuine, lit-up with the desire to paint; all this and more can be seen and read in Paula Modersohn Becker's self-portraits. From the searching, searing earliest paintings to her latest boldest monumental ones, she stands forth before us, the consummate master, casting the essences of her being, her persona, her hopes, her existence into the fabrication of the revelatory fulgent images.

Becker. monotype [touched]. 1978.

Goya

Goya has no equal in savagery. He is the arch expositor of the terror of war, its desolations, its debaucheries, its dehumanizing butcheries. In his "The Disasters of War", teeth of the fresh dead are ravaged for their gold, limbs are haphazardly lopped away, severed heads bedeck shrubs; in the deep densities of black-and-whiteness the marauders in these prints defame and destroy, the rapists rape, the dispensers of plague and horror rage on and on. These etchings invade the precincts of our time, speak to our dread circumstance, are witness to a perpetual sickness, are prophetic of our condition, the drear condition of despair and terror. Goya is relentless. He does not spare himself or us, he spreads before our agonized view scenes of the vilest depredation. He drives his inexorable graphic engine into the hidden realms of our self-cognizance, and into the knowledge of our recent history. They are terrifying images, the ever on-gurgling springs of horror that will not be exhausted, the running sores of our political realities that will not heal, the suppurative cesspool of wars that will not dry out. The Spaniards are the supreme masters of black and white. In that country of blazing sunniness, a backwards-tending church has parched and starved the populace, ensnared it for tortuous inquisitions, for destructive flagellations and for grisly auto-da-fés. The king and his nobility were gloriously attired in the most somber black, the crushing, ruthless, haughty aristocracy added the morose note in that melan-haunted land. Goya sits like his "Colossus" at the dank threshold of our times, he inaugurates our artistic era, he is the newborn artist spewed forth from out of change and revolution, out of incendiary trauma, out of burgeoning nationalism and modernism and out of a changing social order. In a small country house situated in the farther outskirts of Madrid, Goya painted a set of frescos, frightening for their ferocious social ambiguities, for their dense layers of obfuscated meanings; they are in their hugeness and exacerbating oddness called "The Black Paintings". Goya painted them to beguile himself. The fixed, immovable nature of fresco reinforces the private, even secret intention of these works. Goya had moved into the terrifying silences of his deafness; the frescos express those towers of loneliness, those structures of isolation and the stretching, extending,

Goya. etching. 1962.

eternal stillness; see how the "Dog's Head" protrudes into the heavy emptiness of alienation, the demeaning terraces of depression. A horrifying Saturn-like figure devours a remarkably large child; that image must stand for all of us debauching, in our divers ghastly ways, ourselves, our children and our kin. In "Atropos or the Fates", enormous and cretinous Clothe and Lachesis join Atropos in snarling and sniggling the threads of our being; they float over the landscape of our lives, malevolent in their malformations, inharmonious in the juxtaposition of their gross forms. In "Dual with Cudgels" two men, sunk to their knees in a quagmire, furiously fight; in a swampy, empty landscape, they ply their warring clouts, oblivious to their ambience, they sink to the mud, and flay in predacious idiocy. Witches and ancient witch-like crones abound in the Black Paintings; they gyrate, cavort and dance around gross and immense goats or cast themselves about in glistening nakedness, and anthropomorphically prepare to fly off from dank, unwholesome kitchens. The catastrophic "Colossus", with its scenes of bewildering, impending mayhem: the giant brandishes his huge fists in, above, about the cumuli, while far below him a populace madly dashes as though it were part of a Spanish land-grant rush; but the bulls act spell-bound and stampede away from the people. What is happening? One wonders if Goya – except perhaps on a subconscious level – does not fully understand the meaning of the images he proposes to us. Goya is alone in the space he inhabits; no other artist dare trespass his plain of terror, his revelatory steepnesses of human duplicity, his extensive reach into human cruelty, his reason up-ending baring of human depravity. Goya breaks through to the horror of modern times. He is the primal artist of this age.

Postludium

Can one be forgiven the veritable diapason of superlatives that swell
the slack adjectival structures of the forgone writing? Perhaps I should
have undertaken a consideration of artists and works that are of
considerable uninterest and distaste to me. In describing the inanities
and banalities of a Sir William Beechey, the tediums and lacklustrums
of an Anselm Feuerbach, or the insipidities of an Arnold Böcklin or an
Alfred Sisley, to name but four painters of great repute and clout, I
would discover a language of detraction and invective, of vituperative
freshness and of delicious viciousness, which would have provided a
counterweight to the continuous strain of hyperbolic awe and love.
Thus if I were to insist upon and assert the galloping primacy of
Matthias Grünewald over all other artists, the happy balancing
presence of . . . but no one can be as bad as Grünewald is great: that
order of badness is malfeasance, a felonious assault on the
sensibilities, indeed, the senses; the awful perpetrator would not be
countenanced, would forever remain unknown, the work abandoned,
destroyed, or, if truly horrific, elevated like a Norman Rockwell to
veneration and a museum entirely devoted to it; to achieve such
philistinic adoration, the work must perforce be entirely false, of a
ghastly sentimentality and only minimally exist as art. My etched
portrait of Grünewald would more justly sit here if I had the scholastic
baggage to investigate late medieval theological structures in re the
rôle of pain and exacerbation in the assertion of sanctity. And
Grünewald's infinite greatness stilled my smoking pen. Unlike
Rembrandt, onto whose self-portraits and bulging humanness I
clutched and was allowed voyage, Grünewald has no side, no
sentimental protuberances, no irrelevant encumbrance to which I
could attach myself and be carried along in hyperbolic glee and idiocy.
No, there was naught but that awesome Isenheim Altar and its
crescendo of unbelievable panels, painted for solemn contemplation by
lepers and syphilitics and by whoever else was nursed at the hospital
at Aschaffenburg, for which it was painted. I have visited the great
altar four times, now displayed in a museum at Colmar, and each time
I fell into a near swoon of incredulity at its awesome grandeur, its
unassailable heights and depths, its sheer pictorial glory. At its heart

Grünewald. etching [unpublished]. 1954.

hangs the most human of all Christs; he is all over scoured and scourged in blooded red and infested green and suspended in the blackness of suffering. I have seen the Sistine Chapel under ideal conditions and circumstance, the Ghent altarpiece of van Eyck, the Masaccios at the Brancacci Chapel, the Ghibertian doors of Paradise, Rembrandt at the Dutch museums; and nothing can compare to the Isenheim Altarpiece for the depths of its emotional springs, for the complexity of its conceptual correlatives, and for its sheer power and overwhelming beauty. It would perhaps be of confounding interest to consider those artists whom I venerate and of whom I have fashioned portraits but who are absent from these pages, and those I revere but whose portraits I have not attempted. I am forever grading artists on a scale of one to five, an imbecilic gradient of ultimate and penultimate greatness; yet those moronic structures provide me with a kind of trophy-case in which to deck my zealotries in consequent, subsequent and antepenultimate order. Indeed I should keep it a private matter, but it is rather late in this enterprise to veil innermost feelings and attitudes. I have etched the portrait of Lucas van Leyden, an artist I adore for his non-Durerian mode, (I would, in my closet, have said anti-Durerian) and for the essential humanity that shines from his work, which caresses in its avoidance of the histrionic, or of bombast, or of overwhelming technical virtuosity: are Lucas's simpler means the agency by which he touches us? I rather doubt the depth of truth in that expressed antipathy to fustian and technical virtuosity: I love Goltzius, the wizard of the burin and the twirling, whirling excessive machinations of the Haarlem and other Mannerists. I extol the intoxicating inventions of Rosso Fiorentino and Primaticcio and the tenebrosities that dazzle and cloud in the paintings of Bartholomeus Spranger. Why have I not portrayed Rosso, whom I specially admire for his brilliantly neurotic designs for Estienne's "Anatomy", or Spranger the veritable well-head of Northern Mannerism? I have made three still-born portraits of Albrecht Altdorfer, an artist I hugely esteem and who rates near the top, on my assessing scales: the two etchings I made were dismal, hapless, weak failures, as though that Danubian furore and force which inspirit his incredible larches stoppered up my brain and hand. I could find no contemporary portrait of Altdorfer, nor could I find a self-portrait, and I wonder at

208

Wolf Huber's and Lautensacks's non-portrayal of their great colleague. I did publish a tiny wood engraving of Altdorfer, looking, alas, like a rich patron of Hubert or Jan van Eyck, rather than what he was, the painter of the purest magical propensities; whose St Georges are lost into immense, ever up-towering forests, that rise and rise in boundless glory. His martyrs and apostles disport in woods that only flourish in superabundance in Altdorfer's perfervid imagination. In 1525, the town council of Ratisbon (Regensburg today) voted – and Altdorfer was a member of that council – to destroy the ancient synagogue of the town. Altdorfer made two engravings of that doomed synagogue, one of the interior and one of the vestibule with a perambulating sexton, before the destruction could be carried out. The Danubian school were possessed, their works pieced-out in greater or lesser part of enchantment and wonder: there is massive excessiveness in Huber, as though he and Albrecht's brother Erhard and the others were blessed with an over-fecundity, an extra richness of invention, copiousness of fertility; their works are bestrewn with an abandonment of trees, growing in perilous and dizzying splendor. The larches which are abundant along the Danube at Augsburg make in Altdorfer's works a great swoon of draped, uplifted, drooped, and sprung limbs creating aerial canopies, under which angels and putti can sport. I am grieved at Altdorfer's absence from my gallery of favorites, for no artist has granted me greater pleasure and delight especially in the collecting, the possessing and, alas, the selling of his wonderful prints, of which I will only note the woodcut of "St Jerome in his Cave", and what an astonishing woodcut it is. The formschneider, whoever that hand-blessed artisan was, must have cursed Altdorfer to Gehenna and back for having him cut the seemingly endless cross-hatched lines that hold St Jerome in his space penetrating hermitage. That deep skein of lines, characteristic of Altdorfer's woodcuts, defines the saint's ambience; we go deep into the increasing darkness of the cave, we go in so far that magically we begin to go out through excavated walls and a ceiling that subtly filters in the light. A wonderful woodcut, immense in scope, suggestion, possibility and meaning, but relatively small in reality. Altdorfer was a near-visionary, and like all of his kind his humans have that enchanted, balmy look; but his trees swell, cavort and leap, bound,

Altdorfer. we. 1960.

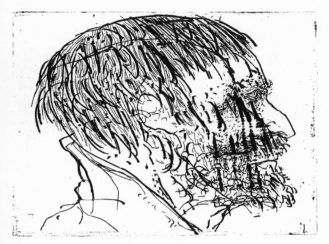

J. Amman. etching [unpublished]. 1963.

vault and skip skyward, caparisoned with deepening greens, bursting into the bluest of heavens. I have not made a portrait of the great Swiss late-sixteenth-century artist, Tobias Stimmer. A draughtsperson of the greatest magnitude, his book of Bible illustrations is a crucial artifact in the development of the Baroque. Rubens went to school with two books, one was the Stimmer and the other was Jost Amman's *Kunstbuchlein*, about which presently. The small woodcuts in the *Neue Kunstliche Figuren Biblischer Historien* depart drastically from the tradition established by Petit Bernard and Hans Holbein, in which the figures and their actions are happily contained within their tiny rectangular spaces: the figures are composed with a sweet harmony of controlled gesture and constrained movement; mildly Mannerist, the small blocks reflect a feeling of Classical resolution and of an ideal achieved. Stimmer sends shafts of wild, discontented, Baroque space into those earlier self-satisfied compositions, the figures violently break out of their encasements, flying and diving and sprawling in their new-found freedom. Rubens copied many of Stimmer's designs in his youth. We own five books illustrated by Tobias Stimmer, two are collections of portraits; looming large and swelling their spaces to bursting point, Jovio's humanists, rulers and soldiers stare out at us and regard us in the bigness of the Baroque vision. A very small octavo has his illustrations for the *Narrenschiff*, as distant from Wolgemut's and Pleydenwurff's and the very young Dürer as can be. A small book of the primal German emperors seen full-length, entirely imaginary, vital and elemental in bearing, and the book of Bible illustrations published at Basel in 1576 by Thoma Gwarin: we have stupidly hearkened to the nonsense that Orson Welles spouts in that film about the Swiss and their cuckoo clocks; Conrad Witz, Hans Holbein, Urs Graf and Nicholas Manuel Deutsch et alia, through to Hodler, Vallaton and Klee, put that lie to shameful rest. Urs Graf and N. M. Deutsch were very violent artists in subject, in mode and, according to tradition, in life; both used a dagger as part of their monograms, and they were privy to its ex-studio uses. They loved to depict prostitutes, *landsknechts*, suicides and battle scenes. They both drew with passion, with a vivid and profuse density of pen marks. Can one readily dismiss that drawing of Dido's self-immolation by Urs Graf? The great heavy pendulous figure crazily careening at a river's

210

edge, the immense dagger piercing her immense abdomen, her face mangled and twisted and startled to a cry; her breasts protuberant, her pudenda rich and vibrant, her buttocks firm; this fleshly suicide is observed from below by an old landsknecht, while a great upstanding tree provides a diverting canopy for the entire scene; a stupendous drawing. And many more admirable and astonishingly original and quite odd drawings by both masters survive. Jost Amman, the Frankfurt am Main artist, is the crucial begetter in several books that I treasure. I have but obliquely portrayed him nor seen him portrayed. In 1556 Sigmund Feyerabend issued Amman's mighty *Kunstbuchlein*, the paragon of model books; it is without text, composed of hundreds of single-page woodcuts, designed by Jost Amman and presumably cut by him. The book sets out to provide artists with the perfected images of everything iconic and pictorial that they were likely to need. The *Kunstbuchlein* was a kind of Artists' ur-morgue. The book abounds in details of costume, images of sultans, Turks and Pharisees in elaborate turbans, instructing provincial and backward painters just how a turban is folded and knotted. Horses of great variety can be found in this book, and in many a prancing and riding position. And saints and martyrs, eremites and sirens, sibyls and mythological beings of all sorts: all drawn in his direct, strong and robust baroque manner. Jost or Jobst Amman is not felt to be a distinct artistic personality. He is generally known and considered an artist given to the carrying-out of the ideas and designs of others; that must, indeed, account for a good deal of his activities and, if no paintings from his hands are known, the *Kunstbuchlein* betokens an artist of great originality, verve and versatility. His path crosses that of a member of that astonishing Nuremberg family of gold and silversmiths called Jamnitzer. Wenzel Jamnitzer issued a volume of perspective, the plates all etched and engraved on metal by Amman. By the 1540s all of the fundamental problems of perspective had long been solved and perspective became a humanistic sport, the plaything of artists, the toy of savants; the Haltens, the Lenckers and the Jamnitzers devised shapes, invented entities, concocted forms of harassing complexity, of eye-wrenching intricacy and brain-twisting convoluted diversity. These objects of geometrical obscurity and architectonic beauty had no other function or purpose than to provide visual models of perspectival problems.

Jamnitzer. drawing. 1987.

These wildly compounded forms were puzzles, which the masters of perspective invented and devised and found delight in their solutions. Uccello and Piero della Francesca invented multi-leveled octagons and objects of other complex shapes, which their new-found knowledge allowed them to draw with convincing realist contours. The multi-leveled brackets and facets and other intricacies became, as time unfolded skill and knowledge, bizarre sculptures of eye- and mind-dazzling complication. Thus Jamnitzer begins with a simple shape and in engraved stages examines the possible variations and changes in structure that can be executed or enacted on it, and they are numerous and intriguing in their subtleties and amazing for their inventiveness. When Jamnitzer exhausts his capacity for variation on the theme of simple to complex, he then invents three-dimensional hedrons and geometricities, extruding onto their surfaces protuberances of every kind, forces these reticulated structures onto their sides, or all askew onto their heads, and even resting on their points or flanges or fins and pushed into confrontational relationships with other strange structures, becoming monuments to the unknown, indeed to the unknowable. In the steadfastness of the forgers of perspective to their tasks, the emergent surreal, weird and bizarre, is apparently overlooked, not considered, possibly not *even* seen as the problem is pursued to its near-insane end. Wenzel's father, uncle or cousin, Christoph Jamnitzer (the family was fecund, and wildly and brilliantly inventive), whatever his relationship, (I do have a complex genealogical table for the Jamnitzers, but as they all tended to be named Wendel or Wenzel or Christoph or Christoffel, and as they all were goldsmiths and engravers, it is a rather difficult tangle to pick apart), issued three sets of prints under the general title of "*Neues Groteskenbuch*" of 1565; he etched the designs and they are delightfully odd, urbanely witty, reaching heights in the invention of unknown creatures, and in the unexpected rearrangement of known animals, reptiles and insects, all comporting, cavorting and moving in unanticipated ways and in their entirety; the three suites of engravings are a fiercely imaginative foray into the worlds of phantasy and phantasmagoria. Of the forty-two artists that bulk-up the ballast of this vessel, only five are sculptors. I regard myself as primarily and essentially a sculptor, so the imbalance is a bit odd. Herewith, then,

212

some tiny disquisitions anent sculptors whose works have moved me. Tilman Riemenschnieder is indubitably the greatest of the late Gothic Lindenwood carvers. Is he greater than Veit Stoss? Titans are titans, they are equally great, but Riemenschnieder touches me all aflutter where Stoss just amazes me. The ensuing why is complex and difficult, and too philosophically grounded to engage my hopelessly non-speculative intelligence. Indeed, why do I prefer Algardi to Bernini, who is universally accorded the greater artist? Is it because Algardi's profound portraits of Philip Neri and Carlo Borremeo are more deeply vested in my consciousness than anything of Bernini's, except for that wonderful "Elephant and Obelisk" and "St Theresa" and the youthful "Louis XIV" and "Urban VIII", which reveals the speciousness of my averral? I was never so witless as to prefer Pater to Watteau or Jordaens to Rubens or Poelenburg to Breenburg; but however great Veit Stoss may be, Tilman Riemenschnieder lives very deep in my heart. I think it very likely, but not in this instance, for a lesser artist to occasionally have a greater effect upon one than a manifestly greater artist. An old legend, restated in a modern novel, has Riemenschnieder taking the peasants' side in their revolt, actively participating in their struggle, in payment for which the archbishops and princes deliberately broke his wonder-working hands, but not before Tilman and those hands had carved altars, figures of saints, Apostles, martyrs, the Virgin and all in abundant combination. The work is shudderingly realistic, and expressive of newly-hatched needs to conquer, to subdue the world, its actualities and its verities. Riemenschnieder is astonishing because his figures suffer no diminution of power, no loss of elemental force; their primal ferociously-present presences are succinctly perceived, they pulse with that late Gothic new-found life. After four hundred years, their powerful theological bulwark does not undermine their quickened vitality; it is intact. How very unlike Donatello Riemenschnieder is; they are near exact contemporaries, but that alien wind that blew the golden dust of ancient Greece and Rome into the awestruck eyes of overcome Trecento and Quattrocento Italians, which permitted Donatello the beauties of nudity and the gestures of an attic-tinged grace and an olympian felicity, denied to Riemenschnieder in the frozen North, who somehow managed, no matter how voluminous

Riemenschnieder. drawing. 1987.

213

Donatello. drawing. 1987.

the fluttering and the encompassing draperies to reveal the divine harmonies of human beings. The burgeoning, ruthless and often coarse Tuscan bankers and princelings did demand of their artist-servitors the visible equivalents, realistically achieved and displayed, of their power and wealth; but by the mid-fifteenth century, under the zealous influence of the Florentine neo-Platonists, levels of subtlety and ambiguity entered the works; works with secret meanings, involving private myths and symbols were produced that were meaningless away from the court. Donatello is influenced by the ubiquitous treasure, found in his immediate ambience and beyond. Donatello is wondrously free of falsehood or sentimentality in gesture and stance, he is never flippant, never irrelevant, nearly always monumental, profoundly poetic and lyric, and his numerous works are free of bombast. Alas, I must own that I prefer Donatello to Michelangelo. I will not undertake a piece-by-piece comparison of works, but will say that it is the very late or the unfinished works of Michelangelo that start me atrembling, whereas virtually all of Donatello's work does, whether the great Zuccone on Giotto's campanile, or the wood-carving of the hirsute, shivering, supplicating ancient crone which was once the sinning beautiful Mary Magdalen in the Florentine Baptistry, or the miraculous low-relief carving of the "Ascension" in the Victoria and Albert, a work whose rhythmic mysteries I yearned to penetrate. Michelangelo is the promethean genius whose works startle, awe and overwhelm us. Donatello is the protean genius, whose works restore us, reassure us, and extend us, his sculptures enlarge our humanness, their harmonies are beguiling, they resonate and they echo in our consciousness and in our memories. Donatello worked in the midst of a great sculptural flowering. It is a pleasure to intone the sculptors' names: the brothers Rossellino, Ghiberti, the della Robbias, Verrocchio, Desiderio da Settignano, Benedetto da Maiano, Mino da Fiesole et alia. Padua in the late fifteenth century and until deep into the sixteenth century was famous for its bronze foundries, and the greatest fashioner of small bronzes was Andrea Riccio; to his hand are attributed a small army of bronze sculptures and placquettes. The possession of small bronzes became a vogue in the late Quattrocento, and was a raging fashion amongst humanists, advanced prelates, and liberated princes. Thus in

214

"St Jerome in his Studio" by Carpaccio, the Saint, as Jennifer Montagu notes is "a fifteenth-century humanist in a room decorated with small bronzes". Of Riccio's numerous works, I will only refer to his remarkable "Horse and Rider" at the V & A. As it is housed in the same gallery as Donatello's "Ascension", I had ample opportunity to study its rampaging, its ferocious energy. This small and miraculous bronze, this raging sculpture, does not betray its essential wholeness, it does not corrupt its forms in meaningless minutiae of harness, equippage and armor; it exerts its powerful qualities of profound alertness and nervous liveliness without the deadly graphic accoutrements of a Remington or a Russell. This magnificent bronze is energized from within, and in some near-mystical way the very bronze seems to throb and shiver with contained explosiveness. Riccio has thrust the hot, exacerbated vitality of life itself into the molten bronze. The "Horse and Rider" is predictive of Giambologna who drives all of Riccio's implications to realizable conclusions. Giambologna is the virtuoso of cast bronze. If Riccio may be counted an artist of the Quattrocento, deriving from that prodigious century, qualities of elemental force and power, then Giambologna can be cited as the artist of the mature Cinquecento, expressing the skills, the finesse and that time's consummacy of finish. By the advent of Giambologna, the rage for "interior bronzes" was rampant and Giambologna fulfilled the need and sated the demand with breathtaking skill and panache. If his sculptures lack the elemental strength of Riccio, they compact a sufficiency of might and force that flows from Giambologna's total formal control. His bronzes radiate these various, captivating qualities; of fluidity: the forms that resolve into a Hercules or into a symbolic "Architectura", drive into one another with a molten mobility and a Mannerist flow of inevitable grace; of exuberance and rich invention of surface: breathtakingly chased by Giambologna, who caused the refined surfaces to be fire-gilded or otherwise brilliantly patinated: of style; the two centuries that spawned them thrust the centrality of each time's style upon each artist. Riccio is stolid, slightly awkward, primordial, thrusting toward an ideal, and is extremely strong. Giambologna is spurred by the Mannerist agitation, his work is elegant, graceful, neurotic, refined and erotic. The response to Giambologna's brilliance was overwhelming and the demand for his

Riccio. drawing. 1987.

Flötner. drawing. 1985.

beautiful bronzes has never ceased. I have never admired Baroque sculpture, the chthonian sculpture of Sumer and Egypt pre-disposed my sensibilities to regard Berniniesque flying forms with displeasure and with suspicion; I will not allow the presence here of any subconscious fear. It has taken me a long time to overcome those primary influences, and I must confess to a certain unease, perhaps imbalance, in responding to great Baroque sculptures: I came to admire Puget through his marvelous drawings, and a quivering admiration for Sebastian Slodtz through a mis-reading of the emotional and intellectual meaning of his "Hannibal"; and I have seen photographs of the mysterious series of wounded soldiers at the Zeughaus by Andreas Schlüter. The deepest reaches of my excited response lie elsewhere, in the works of Peter Flötner, for instance. Flötner worked as a sculptor, was known as "the master of the Apollo fountain", was privy to the covert secrets of very low relief modeling, was one of the Renaissance's greatest masters of ornament and produced a horde of designs for goldsmiths, joiners, engravers et al. Forty of his dazzling designs, flawlessly and intricately cut into wood, were published without title, as a model book for workers in a variety of crafts; some designs are the traditional black on white, but several of the others permit the white to glow in a field of black; at the back of one of the pages is printed, "Gedrucht in Zurych by Rudolf Wyssenbach, 1559." Ten years later these designs appear as culs-de-lampe, reverses and space-fillers in a folio volume of Roman emperors (this book is known for its so-called "Saucer-portraits" because of their huge size and unmitigative roundness): it was published at Tiguri (Zurich) by Andreas Gessnerus. Flötner was but a little master, a divine one, who ranged with total mastery over his staked-out domain and he worked with a beguiling ease. I love the flashing dazzle of white ornament sparkling in a black field, like diamonds sprawled onto black velvet. Historians are in a dither of controversy as to the specifics of attribution, precedence and the like, tending to overlook the spirited originality that flows from his ornament, and the innovative force is readily perceptible in his numerous small placques and in the handful of sculptures that I know. His reliefs tend to depict Biblical or pagan scenes and to consist of series of saints, martyrs, sibyls, and antique deities. He manages in his quite small flat bronzes

216

to reveal spaces of surprising depth and encompassing atmospheres without the blandishments of tone or color or hue. And the trees that flourish in his Ovidian or Canaanite scapes are as much projected traceries of his character and personality as van Gogh's cypresses betray his aspiration and his exhilaration. Flötner's voice is clear and quickly recognizable. A furious poetic intensity, Mannerist in sinuous elongation and vigorously tenable and uprightly visible, flashes from his work; as does an enfolding denseness of plain and forest or cavern and hill in his Biblical and other placques, in which figures appear and as often disappear, or, at least, seem to wander away.

Bartholomeus Spranger was the Mannerist firebrand that set the North all ablaze. That mad Rudolphian extravagance found fertile field in Haarlem, which became the locus genie for Dutch Mannerism. A formidable sodality of painters constelled there. A roll of their memorable names yields a sonorous rumble: Hendrik Goltzius, Cornelius van Haarlem, Joachim Uytewael, Hans van Aachen, Abraham Bloemaert, Jan Muller; I have of necessity strayed from Haarlem to Utrecht and beyond, but they were all Haarlemites withal. And crucial to their subsequent fame was that spirited confraternity of engravers; Matham, Sanraedam, de Gheyn, Cornelius and Frederick Bloemaert et alia. The paintings of these masters are bizarre in subject, wild in gesture, vivid and blatant in color, erotic with persistent nakedness, often multitudinous nudity, shocking in unexpected compositions, beguiling in novel juxtapositions, and always surprising, bold, presumptuous and delightful. The paintings tend to attack one's sensibilities without any refining screens, without the caressing admonitory glazes of muted harmony and contained stillness. Because extreme excess in stance, gesture and composition were typical of them, the Mannerists were perforce pertinaciously proficient in drawing and in perspectival matters; to make believable their incredible imaginings, they required painterly consummacy to project into reality their outlandish inventions; indeed their skills attained the levels of blandishment, as in Goltzius's portrait of Giambologna. The Mannerist passage to believability is revealed, and best perceived, in their wonderful, complex and rich drawings. Jacob de Gheyn is principally appreciated for his drawings and engravings; did he paint? My ignorant memory cannot recall ever seeing a painting by him and one would happily forget Goltzius's wretched paintings, which he wrong-headedly turned to in his old age. Bloemaert's vast drawing skills were revealed and preserved in his famous *Tekiningboek* or drawing manual, skillfully engraved by his sons, which was reissued in innumerable editions, and was gainfully used by countless students and artists throughout Europe. Indeed the drawings of Uytewael are famous for their élan, their vigor, and their masterliness. In no sense do these Haarlem Mannerists form a cohesive whole: they descend from Spranger, they relate, they interact, but each is readily distinguishable from the others. I will not attempt even a slight consideration of their differences, but note the utter impossibility of Uytewael painting that unforgettable "Bathsheba" by Cornelius van Haarlem, or of Cornelius painting Uytewael's clamorous "Marriage of Cupid and Psyche", or anyone but Bloemaert painting that verdant, rhubarb-haunted, enchanted "St John's Preaching in the Wilderness". Bloemaert lived until 1652, dying at the age of ninety. Long before his death perished Dutch Mannerism; the Dutch tremblingly stood at the cusp of the age of Rembrandt, Hals and Vermeer.

It is a futile enterprise, a near impossible endeavor to limn the likeness of Käthe Kollwitz. She was tirelessly interested in her countenance. She was continuously preoccupied in depicting herself and with unstinting zeal, with unwavering intensity and brilliance, constantly probing probity, relentlessly driving her scouring needle and excavating crayon into the geography of her face. Its terrain was minutely explored and it seemed to yield up only one emotional state. Kollwitz's visage is eternally set in deepest gloom. Studies of herself, whether casually drawn or carefully composed and closely worked etchings, all reveal a woman's face trussed into sadness and cloaked in unremittent melancholia. Kollwitz's face became the archetypal face of all of the women in her work. Thus, *she* is the earth-woman clutching to her innermost being the child that lies dead in her arms; when death calls the call is to Kollwitz; the timeless mother turning over the dead on the slaughter-field is Kollwitz, her searching hand is the motherhand of Kollwitz; and it is Kollwitz's child that death is struggling to wrest away from her. Rembrandt and Munch, obsessive self-examiners throughout the years of their lives, were content to abandon their features and their physiognomic body stances when dealing with material of a general or impersonal nature. The universal insistence on appearing and the fabulous presence of Käthe Kollwitz make it hopelessly difficult to portray her without producing either mocking inanity or mawkish sentimentality or, far worse, a trespass into a precious, an exclusive iconography.

C. van Haarlem. drawing. 1986.